SMELLS LIKE
RETIREMENT

SMELLS LIKE RETIREMENT

HOW TO CREATE A ROCK-SOLID PLAN FOR THE BEST YEARS OF YOUR LIFE

Aloha —

[signature]

DONALD J. HURZELER

KUA BAY PUBLISHING

First Edition
ISBN:
Paperback: 978-0-9981063-0-4
Kindle: 978-0-9981063-1-1

THE PURPOSE OF THIS BOOK

A. To get you thinking about your retirement

B. To get you thinking about a retirement that is *extraordinary*, and that becomes the *best* part of your life

C. To give you some tools and ways of thinking that aid decision-making about your future, and get you ready to be retired

D. To give you confidence about your future, so you can greet it with openness and excitement, rather than fear and loathing

E. To give busy people like you a quick read about making retirement decisions

DEDICATION

To our kids, Jim Hurzeler and Stephanie Stanczak. You've made your mom and me the happiest people on earth. We sure enjoyed raising you. We like it even more now that you are adults with families of your own, with all the struggles that will make your eventual victories that much sweeter.

Jim, thanks for upgrading our family by marrying Sarah. And Sarah, thank you for our much-loved grandsons, Sam and Zack.

Stephanie, thank you for marrying Joe, and then adding two wonderful grandkids to the mix. Ava and Nathan may take over the world. They have already taken over our hearts.

Jim and Stephanie, that you have managed to stay so close to each other for all these years, well, it is a parent's dream. Well done. We are proud of you every single day.

Your mom and I love you, and always will.

TABLE OF CONTENTS

CHAPTER ONE

YOU WILL RETIRE.
WHAT WILL YOU DO,
WHERE WILL YOU LIVE,
AND HOW WILL YOU AFFORD IT?

Figuring out what I was going to do in retirement was one of the hardest things I've ever done. It was a real struggle. I am a guy who always has a plan and works it. I make decisions quickly. And yet, when it came to figuring out what my wife and I would do in retirement and where we would live at that time, well, it kind of stumped both of us.

I am one of the lucky ones. I did figure out very early on how to put enough money away for retirement. Money was not my problem, but it is *the* problem for most people, so much so that I've given the situation a lot of thought, and helped quite a few people think through their financial options.

My wife, Linda, retired long ago and had her life pretty well in order. Linda was a happy camper. I was an executive with a large firm. I loved my job and all the travel, and was comfortable being the boss or a member of a team. I, too, was a happy camper. But the calendar kept clicking away, some things changed at work,

I had a long-time promise to myself to save a few years for a writing career, and the time to make a decision was finally on us. It was time to put together a plan and work it.

This book is about the endgame at work, putting a plan together for retirement, executing it, and doing so in such a way that leaves the future open for all kinds of new opportunities and adventures.

CHAPTER TWO

PRE-RETIREMENT CONFUSION

"If you are not confused, you are not paying attention."

Tom Peters

The problem for me may have been too many choices, a host of outside influences, and too little thinking about what might be possible for our lives. The more I became vested in my current life, the harder it was for me to see the additional possibilities. I'll explain.

We've lived in something like a dozen cities during our adult lives. We liked each one: Los Angeles, Chicago, Pittsburgh, Baltimore, New York City, and beyond. We gave serious thought to living in Tokyo and Zurich. Both of us traveled a lot. I often flew more than 100,000 miles a year on business. My wife and I have visited something like 80 countries. After a while, it became a bit confusing. There were so many great places to live. Where would we fit best in retirement?

And then there is the family thing. We started off in California. We are beach people right down to our bone marrow. We love the ocean. We love casual living. We love good weather. We love being near our closest relatives: a son, a daughter, their spouses, and kids. Many of our longest-term friends live in California. California was such an obvious choice. It was also the choice that everyone expected us to make. There was the "opportunities" thing. If we lived centrally in the U.S., it would be easy to consult during retirement, continue some significant volunteer and professional opportunities, accept a few offers to serve on the board of directors of a company or two, promote books I planned to write, and take speaking engagements. In other words, if I just stayed in my existing house and quit working, my wife and I could pretty much continue the life we had, without the bother of having a boss or paying too much attention to the alarm clock.

Oh, and there was the "obligation" thing. No one ever asked us to do so, but we knew that our son and daughter could use our help watching the kids and taking them around to their events. We knew that our aging parents would need our direct help. We knew that my sister occasionally needed our help. We knew we had obligations. Obligations made decision-making difficult.

The very last thing that we considered was this: What do *we* want out of our retirement? That turned out to be a key question. Not what do *others* want us to do in retirement. Not what *must* we do in retirement. Rather, what do we *want* to do in the years ahead?

"One of the great tragedies in life is to lose your own sense of self and accept the version of you that is expected by everyone else."

K. L. Toth

CHAPTER THREE

THINKING IT THROUGH

"Who you are tomorrow begins with what you do today."

Tim Fargo

M y wife and I had to invent this part of our lives for ourselves. After decades of coming to preliminary decisions that we would retire to St. Croix in the Virgin Islands, or Grasse in the south of France, or La Jolla in California, or Las Vegas (OK, that one was all my idea), or Palm Springs in California, or Springdale (just outside of Zion National Park) in Utah, we finally started to see the problem. The problem was that we were trying to pick the place when we should have been trying to figure out what we wanted our life to look like in retirement. Once we looked down that end of the barrel, our plan came together in no time. If we could figure out what we wanted, it would be easy to pick a place that could best accommodate that lifestyle.

This was not a one-session thing, or a checklist to do once and that's it. We did take our time. We revisited our thoughts, we refined them, and then we made a joint decision on the basics of our retirement. To tell the truth, it came together for us only about a year before I retired. I hope reading this book will help you do it a bit more quickly. Once we made those big decisions, we felt like a ton of bricks had been removed from our shoulders. We could get on with making plans and executing them—things we do well.

"Anything is possible. You can always have the life you dream of."

Lailah Gifty Akita

CHAPTER FOUR

TWO QUESTIONS THAT CAN SHAPE YOUR FUTURE LIFE

"So many of our dreams at first seem impossible, then they seem improbable, and then, when we summon the will, they soon become inevitable."

Christopher Reeve

The easiest thing people can do in retirement is make no change at all. In fact, that is the choice many people make. They continue to live in the same house. They may even keep a few clients, or consult, or have an abbreviated workweek. They have more time to do volunteer work. They have more time to help their kids. They may go to Florida for the winter. But their lives remain much the same, just less confined. There is nothing wrong with that. But we wanted something completely different. So we decided to imagine our dream retired life. That led us to the following two questions:

I. What 10 things do we want from our retirement?

We decided to list 10 things that we would love to do on a daily or regular basis in retirement. We did not confine the list to things we could do in our current location. We wanted to explore the ideal situation first. We could always make compromises later. With that in mind, here is the list we developed (in no particular order):

1. **Be warm 365 days of the year.** Perhaps being raised in Southern California, then living for nearly three decades in places like Chicago, Pittsburgh, New York City, and Baltimore influenced us when we made this choice.

2. **Live within 30 driving minutes of a great airport.**

3. **Live within 15 driving minutes of a tropically warm ocean.**

4. **Have Costco, Walmart, or other adequate shopping within a half-hour of our home.** We also wanted good cable TV and fast Internet access. In other words, we did not want to be isolated from modern technology or shopping.

5. **Front-load our retirement so we could do some really adventurous things while we were still physically able.**

6. **Simplify our life significantly.** Move into a new, reasonably sized, one-story, eco-friendly (solar-heated water and solar electric) home, and arrange for contractors or work crews to do most things (for example, I never want to mow a lawn again). We wanted to get rid of most of our possessions, especially those we store in boxes that we rarely open, and organize everything else to simplify things for us and those who will inherit our stuff. We wanted a place that could easily serve us when the time came to hire live-in help to see us through our declining years. We wanted two simple cars, one of which would be a four-wheel drive to take us off the beaten path.

7. **Exercise each day: cardio, stretch, and weights.**

8. **Have time to pursue interests**. I wanted time to write a few books and do some paid speaking engagements. Linda wanted to be involved in a good church and explore her art.

9. **Easily access excellent healthcare**. We wanted to live in an area that could maximize our chances of staying healthy.

10. **Have time to develop or hone our long-neglected skills.** For me, that included golf, surfing, and photography. For Linda, that included art-related interests.

II. What 10 things do we want to avoid in retirement?

We then decided to again be completely honest, and name 10 things we did not want to do in retirement:

1. **Work.** I don't want to work another day for a corporation or in the insurance business. I loved my career, but 40-some years were certainly enough. It was time for me to see what else I could do with my life. That meant no consulting for me.

2. **Volunteer work.** Linda and I had been life-long volunteers. We had given our time and abilities to a number of wonderful organizations, and always seemed to get more out of the work than we put into it. However, we felt it was time to move aside, and let younger people have those opportunities and experiences. From now on, we would give our money, not our time. That meant no more volunteering.

3. **Taking care of people.** This one will not play well in our family, and will show us as the selfish people we intended to become (and are now). We wanted to avoid providing care for our grandchildren, relatives in need, and anyone else. We also decided we did not want pets to tie us down just as we gained total freedom. There may come a time for a pet down the road, but not right now.

9

4. **Running out of money.** So, no Rolls Royce. No second home. No big boat. And, since I love to gamble (including large sums of money), we decided not to live too near a casino.

5. **Living outside the United States.** We've done enough traveling to know that, for us, there is no better place than the United States of America. At the end of the day, we wanted to turn out the lights and know that our home is in America.

6. **Stuff that detracts from our happiness.** As much as possible, we wanted to have fun and be happy, and avoid things that cause us to be angry, irritated, and frustrated.

7. **Segregation.** We did not want to live in a place where everyone looked like us. We wanted diversity in our lives, particularly in age, and cultural and economic status. In other words, we wanted a steady stream of young people in our lives to go along with our older and, possibly, more financially secure friends. And, to be completely candid, we did not want to end up where we were an extreme minority. We wanted to be part of a great mix.

8. **Becoming isolated.** We did not want to become hermits. We wanted to live somewhere our friends and relatives might enjoy visiting.

9. **Becoming disconnected.** We did not want to freeze our view of the world on the day we retired. We wanted to stay current technologically and culturally for the rest of our days.

10. **Becoming a burden on our children and grandchildren.** Some of this may be beyond our control. However, to the best of our ability, we wanted to make life easy for others.

There was nothing sacred about limiting the list to 10 things. As you can see, we crammed a lot more than 10 things into the lists. However, we did not want the lists to get so long that they became confusing. So we settled on 10. You may want a dozen. It is up to you.

Putting a Face on Our Retirement

The above exercise gave a face to our proposed retirement lifestyle. Linda and I did not agree 100 percent on each item. Neither of us thought we would be able to make every single one of the ideas come true. However, we did believe our dreams were now on the table. We believed those dreams could inform our decision-making about where we wanted to live in retirement.

By the way, if you have always lived by putting the dreams and ideas of others before your own, when are you going to speak up and be heard? This is the time to finally give wings to your ideas. If you can't say your dreams out loud in front of others or write them down for all to see, they will not happen. This may be your last chance at true happiness. Speak up and at least get your thoughts/ideas/dreams/emotions on the table for consideration. You are every bit as important as your partner or whoever else is influencing your retirement decisions. Blurt out the truth, and see where the conversation takes you. It could lead to the happiest days of your life.

One more thing. Linda and I agreed that life changes over time, and no decision we made now would be good forever. We articulated an exciting future for ourselves but fully realized that it was just the start of a journey. The next stop on the journey was figuring out a place to live that would accommodate our proposed new lifestyle.

> *"You have to leave the city of your comfort and go into the wilderness of your intuition. What you'll discover will be wonderful. What you'll discover will be yourself."*
>
> Alan Alda

CHAPTER FIVE

A CLEAN-SLATE LOOK AT
WHERE YOU WILL LIVE

*"All men should strive to learn before they die,
what they are running from, and to, and why."*

James Thurber

Your choices fit into one of eight categories:

- Stay where you are, and maybe buy a timeshare or a place in Florida for your winter home.

- Move to where your kids live.

- Move into a retirement community.

- Move to a place that looks perfect, and ignore some obvious problems, because you want the lifestyle it offers but cannot afford to live that way in a more conventional location. This is how U.S. retirees end up in Mexico, Costa Rica, or the Ozarks.

    Before you get pissed off at me, I must say I love all three locations and visit them often. However, if I had the money to live where I wanted, I would continue to visit these places, but not live in any of them. Why? Mexico is becoming increasingly dangerous and does not have the kind of infrastructure I want to support me in retirement. Costa Rica is located between two problematic countries and is prone to natural disasters. I just don't want to live in the Ozarks. That area is not close to the ocean.

- Get a motor home, and head off to see the world.

- Disappear. Hermit time. A few people move so far away from everything that, for all intents and purposes, they are hermits.

- Move back home to the area where you grew up, or to a place you once lived and still love.

- Move to a place where you've never lived that might accommodate the kind of lifestyle you envision in retirement.

My suspicion is that most people aren't willing to explore these ideas. Most have already made up their minds long before retirement (as in: We will keep this house, and buy a condo in Florida for the winters). Their decision is such a no-brainer that they don't want to spend even a minute considering anything different. And if I am right, those people miss one of the greatest opportunities of their remaining time. They miss the chance to put their dreams on the table for careful consideration before deciding where to make them come true.

This may be a really easy decision for you. If it is, please give it one more hard thought after doing the exercise "What 10 things do we want from our retirement?" It will better serve you to do that exercise first, rather than decide where to live, then see what aspects of your dreams you can salvage in that place. Where you live will drive what you can do on a daily basis.

So here is what we did to determine where we would live. It was one of the hardest decisions of our lives, and has brought us more happiness than any other choice we've made in retirement.

Our top 10 lists (things we wanted and wished to avoid) helped us narrow down the possibilities rather quickly.

- The west coast of the U.S. was out, because the ocean is cold and the weather is not great 365 days a year. It's great most of the time, but not all the time.

- Desert areas like Las Vegas and Phoenix were out, because I often seem to get colds in desert communities, including Southern California.

- We were living in Chicago at the time of our retirement and ruled it out, along with dozens of other states, because of the weather and the absence of a warm ocean.

- Both of us love to visit Florida, but felt it was too crowded and too flat. (We love the mountains.)

- The southern states were out, because of weather and the absence of a year-round warm ocean.

- Alaska was out. We love Alaska, but it did not fit most of our criteria.

- The East Coast was out. We could not use the ocean as we wanted for surfing, snorkeling, and just plain swimming every day of the year and without a wetsuit.

- Some of the places we love were out, because they were not part of the United States: the Virgin Islands (a U.S. territory—close, but not the same), the South of France, Costa Rica, Uruguay, and Chile, to name a few.

What was left? Hawaii was left.

Now, this is not a commercial for living in Hawaii. In fact, I really don't think Hawaii is a good choice for most people. But it turns out to be a great choice for us. The weather is pretty much the same every day of the year—sunny and 84 degrees with some showers in the afternoon. The ocean is around 80 degrees all year long, and the surfing and snorkeling are fabulous. Hawaii is in the U.S.A. It really is.

Hawaii is a large place. Where would we live in Hawaii? We knew it wouldn't be in the northern part of the chain of islands. People really don't live there. People live in Oahu, Maui, Hawaii, Lana'i, Moloka'I, or Kauai. So we looked at our lists and started to see whether we could narrow things down even further.

- Lana'i and Moloka'i are sparsely populated and do not have some things on our lists—for example, an international airport, a Costco, and great healthcare. We decided they were too remote for us, and not a good fit as our retirement home. We love to visit them, and can easily do so from our current location.

- Oahu is fabulous, but way too crowded for what we wanted. Not a bad choice, but we thought we could find a better one.

- Maui is beautiful and it has much of what we wanted on our lists. However, it is kind of expensive. We thought we could do better elsewhere.

- Kauai is beyond beautiful, but a bit small for our tastes. The ocean conditions there are a bit more challenging than we might safely enjoy on a daily basis. We looked at one more island.

- Hawaii—the Big Island. We know this island well. Linda's grandparents lived on the Big Island. We've been visiting it since 1970. We took our kids there. I took my folks there. My sister was there long ago, maybe twice. The surfing vibe is good. The ocean is crystal clear and warm. The coral is in great shape. There are two volcanoes that are both nearly 14,000 feet tall and several others that range from 4,000 feet to 8,000 feet. Hawaii has every climate you can think of within an hour or two of driving from any point on the island, from too hot right down on the beach, to too cold in the winter snow of Mauna Kea or Mauna Loa. In short, it has everything we wanted on our lists except one big item. The healthcare on the Big Island is not world class. At the time of our retirement, the Big Island did not have all the modern medical equipment and specialists that an aging person might need. A problem, indeed.

We had it narrowed down to the Big Island of Hawaii, noting the one scary problem. Now what? Well, here is what we did.

We decided to continue to live in Chicago for the first year of our retirement, and lease a condo on the Big Island of Hawaii for the period of November to April. I was going to retire on June 1, so that gave me time to do a few things before making a life-changing decision.

- We took a "sorbet" month (more about this in a later chapter) to convince ourselves we really had retired and things had actually changed for us.

- I played golf until my hands bled. I'd always wanted to be able to do this. I'd always thought I could become a scratch golfer. It turns out that I had been delusional. I did play my fill of golf. I never got better but loved trying.

- I had time for my "put-off-forever" projects. More about that later.

- I wrote my second book.

- We took our first two month-long trips: one to Utah and one to Australia.

Linda's life didn't change much during this time. In fact, perhaps it got worse. I had been gone several days a week on business travel for the past few decades. I was now around the house 24/7. It turns out that she kind of runs our home and did not really need another house CEO to help her.

But then things got better. November arrived, and we were off to the Big Island for six months.

If you decide you are going to move to a place that looks like it might best accommodate your desired retirement lifestyle, I highly recommend you give it a really good try before actually taking the plunge. We learned a lot during our first winter in Hawaii. The first thing we learned: We never wanted the six months to end. The next thing: Not everything was perfect in Hawaii, so we started to learn how to work around what needed to be addressed. The third thing: If we really wanted to fit into Hawaii long term, we had better abandon some long-held habits and form some new ones. We were up for the challenge on all counts.

We did return to Chicago. We started the difficult process of downsizing and simplifying our lives. We got rid of maybe half to three-quarters of our worldly goods. We gave most of them away to friends, relatives, neighbors, people in need, and charities. The rest of the stuff, we took to the dump. I must say, I do not miss a single thing we got rid of during that time. It was a real relief to not be burdened by all the stuff we had accumulated in our 40 years together. A few tears. For example, giving up a beloved sago palm. Hey, we even managed to package up all of the stuff we had saved for our kids and deliver it to them to do with as they wished. Wow. What a great move that was.

In the end, we had 20,000 pounds of stuff left (OK, so we didn't get right down to the bare bones) and two cars we wanted to take with us. But we couldn't make the move just yet. I had a book coming out and needed to be on the mainland to promote it. And we had not sold our house in Chicago or found a house in Hawaii.

We did another winter in Hawaii, and this time we nearly fell apart on the day we had to return to Chicago. Our hearts were now in Hawaii. We got our house in Chicago ready to go on the market, and returned for another long trip to Hawaii.

The day we arrived in Hawaii for our third long stay, we bought a house. That sale fell apart when the greedy builder refused to come down to our generous half-off offer. We then found another house—this one a "project." It was on a short sale. It was maybe 80 percent complete. It had stood abandoned and incomplete for something like two years. It looked a mess, but had good "bones" and a great view. It was offered at "bank-approved pricing." We offered "Hurzeler-approved pricing." We got the house. We camped out in it twice with good friends: first with Karin May and then with Dan Fairbanks. We lined up the contractors to finish and repair the house to our specs, and headed back to the mainland to go on a book tour. Once the book tour was over, we had a mover pack up our household goods and ship them to Hawaii. We drove our cars (filled with things for the kids) out to L.A. and dropped the stuff off to the combined chorus of, "Where are we going to put all this?" Then we drove our cars down to the dock to be shipped to Hawaii.

When we arrived in Hawaii, and much to our amazement, the contracted work had been done perfectly and far exceeded our expectations. We moved in on blow-up beds, and with a few drinks and food in a couple of coolers. There was nothing to do now but wait for our stuff to arrive by ship. A couple of weeks passed, and the goods and cars showed up in perfect shape. We were ready to get on with our completely new life.

This was a long way around to the important points:

- **Let your dreams for your retirement guide where you will live.**

- **Use those dreams to help inform your search and narrow it down to a place that is highly likely to accommodate your proposed new lifestyle.**

- Wrap up loose ends, get ready for your new home, and prepare to make the big move (or not, if that is your decision).

- Test out your decision before you make a full-on commitment. Try living in the new way, or place, before you actually move.

- And remember that no move has to be your last. People, circumstances, and events change our lives. You can always put your stuff in a truck or on a boat and move again.

And one last thing: No decision or move will be without some challenges. Work around the problems and make it happen.

"If you really want something, you can figure out how to make it happen."

Cher

CHAPTER SIX

WHAT IF YOU AND YOUR SPOUSE
WANT POLAR OPPOSITE THINGS
IN RETIREMENT?

"Compromise is what binds people together.
Compromise is sharing and conciliatory,
it is loving and kind and unselfish."

Ali Harris

Tough one. Not sure I have a great answer. I do know this after being married to the same woman for over 47 years: Married life is often about compromise. There are bound to be several things on the list of things you want from retirement (and don't) that match—areas for total agreement. That is always a good start.

As to the things that are 180 degrees different—here's an example.

"I want to stay here in Cleveland and do unpaid daycare for our grandkids until they reach high-school age," says your wife. You say, "I want to move to Fiji and surf daily, all day long." Oh, this one is not going to go well. Maybe you can agree to do it her way now and get your wish next year. Maybe you can get a pass to head to Fiji a couple of months a year while she takes care of the kids. For better or worse, you are going to have to look for middle ground and some way to accommodate each other's wishes. I wish you the best of luck.

Worst-case scenario: One or both of you totally give up on your dreams. A partially realized dream is always better than no part of the dream coming true. If you made it this far in your marriage, you will work it out. Talk it out. Compromise. Look for middle ground. Things change as time goes by. Once in a while, you just have to bide your time and wait for the other person to see the light. Maybe you have to wait for your own light to go on.

"It is time to recognize what compromise means: no side wins or loses all."

Madeleine Kunin

CHAPTER SEVEN

RETIREMENT PREP—
AND I DON'T MEAN THE WEEK BEFORE
YOU ACTUALLY DO IT

*"Sadly, retirement planning, in many circumstances,
has become nothing more than planned procrastination."*

Richie Norton

Most of us have such busy lives that we give very little thought to our retirement or just don't want to even think about it. One of my best friends at my last job was the chief operating officer of the multi-billion-dollar firm for which I worked. I loved this guy. He was a hands-on guy, and his plate was full. I knew that he was coming up on 65 years of age, and that our company rules would require him to retire. So one day, armed with several books I had bought for him, I ventured into his office to have a talk about doing some retirement planning. He said, "I am so tired, overworked, and out of energy, that all I can do is kind of stumble toward the finish line and wind up my career. I have no capacity whatsoever for even something as important as retirement planning. Thank you for caring, but just let me finish this off, and we can talk when I am out of here."

He had taken some steps to plan for his retirement. He had a wealth management firm look at his finances and, I believe, get his legal documents (like a will) in good order. But as for what he was going to do next—no time for that now.

All of the above became a moot point, because my good buddy found out during his first week of retirement that he had a rare form of cancer and died about two years down the road. Much of his "retirement" was filled with medical-related procedures and examinations. That sucked.

Why do I bring up this story? I bring it up to use my friend as a bit of an example. He was extremely well-educated—one of the smartest people I've ever met. He had a fabulous income and a great family. He had spent his entire working life around strategic planning. And yet, this brilliant guy made it all the way to his retirement day without putting together a plan for himself and his wife. So, if you find yourself staring down the barrel of an upcoming retirement and have not given your future life an adequate amount of thought, you are not alone.

Maybe that is what you want to do during your first few months of retirement when you have the time to devote to it. If so, cool. However, your mortality clock is clicking away, and I am in favor of getting a running start. Tick tock.

Interesting fact: The average American retiring at age 65 has fewer than 20 years left to live.

So whatever your situation, get on with it. A bit of planning now can really pay big dividends during your retirement. Now is the time.

"As in all successful ventures, the foundation of a good retirement is planning."

Earl Nightingale

CHAPTER EIGHT

THINK YOU KNOW HOW MUCH MONEY YOU WILL HAVE FOR RETIREMENT? HAVE YOU READ THE FINE PRINT?

"Nothing in fine print is ever good news."

Andy Rooney

I will admit that I was not a genius when it came to paying careful attention to all things financial related to retirement. Retirement always seemed so far off, and the illustrated figures always looked so wonderful that I failed to really examine the details. When I did, I was shocked. I had quite a bit less money for my retirement than I had counted on. Oh, it got way worse. I retired in 2008, took much of my money in lump sums, invested heavily in the stock market, and then watched the bottom drop out while I was trying to enjoy my first long international trip to Australia.

What do I mean by "read the fine print?" Well, I found that almost every retirement vehicle I had in place had some odd tax regulation or other rule that diminished how much economic value was headed my way. In one case, I was actually owed more money than I had planned on. Here is a brief summary.

- I retired at 61 and decided to take my Social Security benefits at age 62, not because it was a smart thing to do, but I had a couple of nasty bouts with cancer and, by gosh, I was going to start getting that retirement payment as early as possible, just in case. The rules that affect how much you get from Social Security are well-known, but also well worth revisiting. I found the Social Security Administration to be the most professional, best-run, most user-friendly government operation I have ever encountered (their website is fabulous and so easy to use that I never had to visit one of their offices). But it still made a couple of mistakes in how much I would be paid. I used its own formula, filled in my numbers, and found that it had made a small mistake—not in my favor. The Social Security Administration corrected the mistake immediately. Later, it questioned my income and demanded a refund of the money I had received. It took me three phone conversations, but I found reasonable people who took the time to understand my situation and agreed that they had made a mistake. They corrected it immediately. And later, when my wife filed for Social Security online on a Friday, we just about fell out of our chairs when they called us the next day, Saturday, to go over the application. They helped my wife qualify for the most amount of money she was owed. I love the Social Security Administration. However, trust but verify. The devil is in the details. Don't just accept any number or ruling thrown your way. Make sure it is right. And, happily, the Social Security employees seem to genuinely want that number to be right for you.

- I had a lump sum coming to me. Instead of accepting a monthly retirement check, I chose to take the net present value of that "annuity," then invest that money on my own.

You have to be careful with lump sums. If they are not handled correctly, you can trigger a tax event that will immediately wipe out about 40 percent of your lump sum. Get some help with handling lump sums.

I got the money. Then I read that the company had incorrectly figured out others' lump sums, and the amounts were *not* in favor of the retirees. A few had been successful in getting the formula, inputting their own figures, and finding the correct amount owed. This happened enough times that the company stood prepared to do the recalculation on request. I requested. Net result: a check for nearly $100,000 more. Yippee. Trust, but verify. The devil is in the details.

- Some of this I should have known without reading the fine print but didn't. I guess the numbers looked so good, I didn't want to know anything more about them. My mistake. Case in point: I qualified for an executive annuity on top of my retirement payout. I was to receive a large amount of money, in the form of monthly payments, for the rest of my life. Cool. I loved it. Now comes the fine print. Oh, you want that payment to continue for your wife after you croak? Well, that will reduce the amount of the monthly annuity by—technical term coming up—a shitload. I never counted on that one. Oh, and did you know that you have to pay certain taxes on the full calculated value of the annuity, right now, in full, even if you don't live to see payment number two? I did not. Out the window went something like $35,000 before I was ever paid a penny. Ouch.

- I had an executive savings plan. I knew how much I had in that plan, and what was vested, that would come my way when I retired. I guess I knew, but had not thought about the fact that the company had paid into that plan a certain amount that was fully taxable on retirement. By the time the company had gotten around to cashing me out (I don't recall their warning me) of enough of that invested plan so they could send the government the money I owed in taxes, the bottom had dropped out of the market, and I was—another technical term here—screwed. The devil is in the details.

- I was smart about how I treated the money in my IRA account. Now would be a great time to remind yourself of the IRA, Roth, and Keogh plan rules. As I said before, you do not want to trigger a tax event.

- There may be decisions you will have to make on when, and how, to take various retirement plans or vehicles. Get with experts early on. You don't want to make those important decisions a few days prior to retirement while sitting in the office of the human resources person who has been assigned to your case.

- If you are fortunate enough to have restricted stock or options, know before you go. You will find all kinds of rules in place that can affect the value of those shares.

- Same for any bonus plans, profit-sharing plans, vacation accruals, and the like. Know before you go, so you can have some time and leverage to bargain before you are out the door. Once you are out the door, good luck bargaining. I came into the office where I had once been a CEO/president the day after I retired and was given a huge "visitor" badge to wear. Someone was assigned to escort me through the building. I was not feeling very powerful at that point.

- Also in the category of "know before you go": Ask about such things as company cars. Can you buy yours for a song and a dance? Can you continue to use the company-arranged discounts once you are retired? Can you take your laptop with you? Can you continue to use the workout facility for the 10 bucks a month employees pay? You don't ask, you don't get. My basic thought was this: You keep the office plants, and I want everything else. Worth a try.

- Depending on how you go out the door, at least check and see if you qualify for unemployment payments. Unlikely, but worth a try. You paid in for them. Why not get them if you are legally entitled?

- And aren't there some lovely parting gifts they give retirees? Where is mine? Can I just get the cash rather than that nifty set of binoculars you plan to order for me? The point is, if you plan ahead, maybe you can get the cash.

Know before you go. The earlier, the better. Trust, but verify. Don't just take what is handed to you. Check it out yourself. You don't ask, you don't get. Anything you see that is not tied down, see if you can take it with you. And finally, cash is better than goods or services. Try to get everything offered to you on the way out the door *in cash*. Cash is good.

"Do you know the difference between education and experience? Education is when you read the fine print; experience is what you get when you don't."

Pete Seeger

,

CHAPTER NINE

YOU WILL NEED MILLIONS.
THAT IS THE PLURAL OF "MILLION."

*"The question isn't at what age I want to retire,
it's at what income."*

George Foreman

Do you remember the two important words on the back cover of the book *The Hitchhiker's Guide to the Galaxy*? They are: "DON'T PANIC." You will need millions of dollars (with an "s" on the end of "million"), but I am betting you have that kind of money, even if you don't realize it. For now, don't panic, and we will come directly back to this point after a story or two.

One of the saddest things I've ever heard was told to me by a colleague from South Africa. We were together in Europe for a meeting. He asked me when I thought I would retire. I told him I had always planned to retire when I was 62, sooner if I could, and that I had other things I wanted to explore in life. I asked him the same question. He said, "They are going to make me retire at age 65." I asked him if he loved his job so much that he could not stand the idea of retiring. "Hell, no," he replied. "I just don't have any money to retire." He went on to tell me that his retirement plan (or was it his own planning?) was so poor that, at best, he could only hope to join up with some of his friends once a year and caravan around his beautiful country for a week. The rest of the time he would spend at home, working some small job for a little extra money.

This guy was a senior technician for a very large company, and had worked solidly for 40 years. How did this happen?

DON'T GET CAUGHT SHORT

It happens all the time. I cannot count the number of very emotional people who came into to my office to tell me basically the same story.

"Don, I am 50 years old. I've earned way over a $100,000 a year for as long as I can remember. I've traveled the world and enjoyed the best of everything, and now I am 10 to 15 years away from retirement and have less than $25,000 saved up." That is usually when the tears begin—theirs and mine.

The downside of not accumulating enough money for retirement is a lifestyle that gets smaller and smaller over time. An anxiety level that becomes higher and higher over time. Resentment with the government and corporate America that builds up as your financial situation deteriorates. In some cases, you actually get robbed of what I feel is your God-given right to quit working and enjoy life. You end up taking low-paying jobs because you find that's all that are available to you when you hit 65, 70, or higher.

I am, unfortunately, not disgustingly rich at this point in my life. I am, however, financially secure. I got that way by putting away as little as 5 percent of everything I have ever earned and as much as the law would allow in a tax-protected vehicle like a 401(k). I did it every week, week after week, for 40 years. I invested the money semi-wisely and never withdrew a penny. I don't plan to withdraw a penny until I am 70-and-a-half, when I am required to withdraw at least 5 percent of that money each year until it is gone. It will never be gone. And it will make my last couple of decades on this earth financially quite comfortable.

And now that I have been retired for something like eight years, I can start to see clearly how much money it really takes to retire. That might be of interest to you if you are preparing to retire at age 55 and think you have enough money to see you through, or if you are 61 and still have several more years to earn big money before you retire. If you are 65, it is what it is. No amount of planning is going to give you a lot more money for retirement.

YOU NEED MILLIONS TO RETIRE.
THAT IS THE PLURAL OF "MILLION."

You will need way more money than you think to retire in style. Way more money. Millions. I am not kidding. You will need millions.

The first person I showed this to nearly had a heart attack as he read these words. He also strongly disagreed with me. He pointed out two things. First, that money is not necessarily the key to happiness and second, that lots of people get by on way less than a million dollars. Of course, he is right. However, he missed the point a bit. **This book is about getting what you want in retirement**. It is not about making the best of what you have. Of course, I would say if you have only Social Security to live on in retirement, learn to use our libraries, parks, city facilities, and this great, big, beautiful world of ours to find happiness. And if that truly makes you happy, and you want for nothing more, God bless you.

Oh, by the way, if you earn about $24,000 a year from Social Security, let me point out that it would take $1,000,000 invested relatively aggressively (these days) to earn 2.4 percent in a dividend or interest to give you that kind of retirement income. So, in fact, you already have the equivalent of $1,000,000 in retirement assets. Say your wife earns about the same from her Social Security payments. So, adding the two payments together, you and your wife start off with the income flow from about $2,000,000 in retirement assets. Last time I checked, $2,000,000 qualifies in the range of the plural of million. Two million is "millions," with an "s" on the end.

I then asked my friend if that combined income of $48,000 a year was enough for him to have, and do, everything he *wanted* to do in retirement. His answer: "No." He needed even more per year to live on, and to do, the things he wanted—maybe twice as much income. So I rest my case. Millions, indeed.

So, don't panic just yet. You may be looking at things differently than I do. When I say millions, I am talking about either having the assets to produce the annual cash flow needed to finance the lifestyle you want in retirement, or being entitled to things like Social Security, or a company pension, or annuities, or other income stream that will allow you to live as you choose. I do not mean that you must have multiple millions of dollars in a bank account somewhere, though that would be nice.

There are tricks, gimmicks, and one-off tax issues that can make your retirement planning that much more difficult. You will need to get really good at looking at numbers and understanding exactly what they mean.

My guess is you may have no idea how much money you actually need to retire. How much will you need if you retire at 60, before Social Security kicks in? How much will you need after age 70 and one-half, when you must start withdrawing from your 401(k)? And what are the answers to such questions as:

How much do you want left over for your children or charity? **How much do you want in reserve just to make damn sure you never outlive your money?** What is your alternate plan if an important part of your retirement income disappears in the stock market, through a pension plan that goes belly-up, or because of unexpected expenses? If you don't have really crystal-clear answers to the above questions, how are you going to plan effectively for your retirement?

Let's start with the first part, that it is going to take millions to retire in a financially secure manner. How come so much?

YOU WILL NEED INCOME-GENERATING ASSETS AND/ OR FINANCIAL STREAMS. BOTH ARE GOOD.

Well, there is some good news. You need millions or the income equivalent. For example, if a husband and wife will earn $3,000 a month total from Social Security, that is $36,000 a year. You would have to have saved up, and invested, about $1,500,000 on your own to have that rate of return (don't call the accounting police on me—I am rounding for the sake of example). Let's say you feel you need another annual $64,000 to live like you want in your golden years, for an income of $100,000 a year before taxes. Well, maybe between the two of you, you have corporate pensions that will pay another $50,000 a year. Thank God, because you would need to have invested about $2 million of your own money to provide that kind of an income stream (I used a 2.5 percent rate of return, which would provide you an annual $50,000 before taxes). That still leaves $14,000 a year to earn from your own investments, which would need to total about $500,000.

YOU CAN DRAW DOWN SAVINGS
UNTIL THEY ARE COMPLETELY GONE

I explained earlier that you will probably need millions in retirement assets (either those that earn, or entitlements like Social Security that provide an income stream) to finance the lifestyle you want, as opposed to one that lets you just get by.

I know that many people also draw down savings, or choose an annuity that provides earnings on the investments and part of the principle, until, in theory, all of the money is paid out, and the guarantor has to keep payments coming until you die. In these cases, there may be no money left to pass on to the next generation. In drawing down savings, you will have to be really good at predicting your death date so you die at just the right time to make it all work out.

The reality is, it may be too late for you to do anything but draw down your savings to pay for the lifestyle you want. That lifestyle just won't provide the same amount of security about outliving your money. It won't provide the satisfaction of knowing that you will leave something for your children, grandchildren, or charitable cause. And it might mean you approach retirement with a lot more financial caution than you exercised during your working years. If that is the case, it is not the end of the world. Accept reality and find the happiness that is out there for you despite your financial situation.

"You can be young without money but you can't be old without it."

Tennessee Williams

CHAPTER TEN

PUT A PENCIL TO YOUR IDEAL SPENDING PLAN

"He who knows that enough is enough will always have enough."

Lao Tzu

How much will you need in income each year when you retire? That is not as easy to figure as you might think. Your retirement income needs at age 62 are much different from what they will be at 92. For the purposes of making this simple, I am going to build a plan that you can then cut in half, double, or triple to meet your own needs. Here it is.

You can get software to help you do this with some degree of precision. This is just a rule of thumb for getting a gross estimate of what you will need.

Figure out the big buckets of expenses, then make a generous, high-end estimate of how much you want to spend.

Example:

ITEM	MONTHLY	ANNUAL
FOOD All food and drink including restaurants	$750	$9,000
CLOTHING New clothes and dry cleaning	250	3,000
HOUSING Payment or rent, all insurance all taxes, repairs, utilities, association fees, club fees	1,000	12,000
AUTO Two cars, all gas, repairs, insurance licenses, stickers	333	4,000
VACATION Enough for a couple of great trips each year plus regular entertainment	500	6,000
PHONE/CABLE Home and cell phones and Internet	250	3,000
NEW STUFF Any new items except cars, homes, or clothes	250	3,000
REPAIRS For anything except homes or cars	250	3,000
DONATIONS Church and other out-of-pocket cash items	250	3,000

ITEM	MONTHLY	ANNUAL
MISCELLANEOUS Stuff like haircuts, golf, magazines	500	6,000
SURPLUS Good idea to build up some surplus to pay for unexpected big-ticket items	250	3,000
HEALTHCARE Includes heath insurance and out-of-pocket expenses	1,000	12,000
CARE FOR OTHERS Includes taking care of a parent or relative	250	3,000
GIFTS Includes money you wish to pass to a relative tax-free, and all other gifts for Christmas and so on	250	3,000
TAXES You probably have to pay state and federal taxes on your income as it is earned or taken out of your IRA. Does not include house tax, included under "HOUSING."	2,250	27,000
TOTALS	$8,333	$100,000

Add or subtract buckets or change the figures to meet your needs.

Alrighty, then. You have figured out that you can retire quite nicely, and with a large degree of financial security, on the above amount or some variation. Now, how do you put a plan in place to get you financially ready for retirement?

Here is one lesson learned the hard way. There will *always* be some horrible and completely unexpected expense that comes at just the wrong time each and every year. Your car falls apart, or you need a lawyer. There are other uncovered expenses like medical or dental, or a funeral. No one ever plans for these. People act like these experiences are unique to them. If you really want to do a good job of planning, create a budget for the unexpected. There will come a day when you will be thankful you did this extraordinary planning.

"How ridiculous and how strange to be surprised at anything which happens in life."

Marcus Aurelius

CHAPTER ELEVEN

GET YOUR FINANCES IN ORDER BEFORE YOU RETIRE—AN EIGHT STEP PROGRAM

"The time to repair the roof is when the sun is shining."

John F. Kennedy

Step One: Save as much as you can for as long as you can. Don't let anything distract you from putting this money away. Never stop saving, and don't ever withdraw money for something like a house purchase. You will need to be steely-eyed about constantly saving your money over a long period of time.

Step Two: Hold those savings in a tax-deferred plan such as an IRA.

Step Three: Invest the IRA in a mutual fund tied to the Dow Jones or S&P stocks.

There is no completely safe way to invest your money, so you have to go with the odds. The odds will show you that the greatest return over the past 40 or so years has come from investing money across the entire Dow Jones or S&P stock portfolio. Lots of ups and downs, but a good return over time.

The next steps get you ready to actually retire.

Step Four: Pay off all credit cards and other debts.

The sooner, the better. What would really be cool is if you found a way to live your life without any debt along your journey. I couldn't do it. I hope you can. If you ever find you have extra or unexpected cash, and you need to decide whether to spend it by paying off credit cards, investing it, or paying off the mortgage, pay off the credit cards. Most credit card debt is high-interest, which is usually not tax-deductible. Pay off credit card debt.

Step Five: Pay off the house, and don't listen to those who tell you that you need a tax deduction.

If you can afford to do so, change to a 15-year mortgage. You'll get you to your financial goals a whole lot quicker and more cheaply than with a 30-year one. Or you can pay an extra $100 a month toward the principle of the loan, or pay it down every time you get a bonus. Do anything you can to pay the mortgage down quickly.

Once you have your house paid for, you are golden.

Step Six: Figure out how much investment income you need to live on comfortably, not cheaply, for the rest of your life.

You will live on the investment income and *never* touch the principle. That strategy gives you a safety net, frees you from financial worry, and provides an inheritance for those you love. Use the simple budgeting example above to give you a rough idea of how much cash you will need each month to live comfortably in retirement.

One bonus: You can probably reduce the amount you need to live on at certain points in the future. For example, you probably need less money to live on at age 80 than you do at 62. Even less at age 90, but then those pesky medical bills may start to add up—assisted living and the like. By the way, I figure all of my financial scenarios based on my belief that I may live to be 100. If I die sooner than that, the kids (who will no longer be kids at that point) get more money. If I live past 100, I'm guessing I will be a burden to the family or society, and I'm not worrying about it anymore.

Step Seven: By now, you are close enough to retirement that you can calculate, with some certainty, the sources of your income, and how much you will have each month. Make that calculation.

AN IMPORTANT ASIDE: This may be a great time to meet with a retirement planner, or wealth management person or team at your bank. You may have to spend some money on this, but it will be worth it. They will confirm your figures, provide great ideas on handling upcoming events for tax purposes, and may even design investment strategies for you. I am not a big fan of letting someone other than myself manage my finances, but that is because I have the tools and knowledge to do it. If you do not, get some help. Stick with real professionals, and check credentials. It is not a good idea to trust your entire future financial well-being to a friend, relative, or someone from your church or civic club who wants your business, but doesn't really have the background or backing to do a great job. Trust, but verify, and don't turn over your finances to anyone unless you absolutely have to because of poor health or other significant circumstances.

BIG-TIME WARNING!

Two red flags for me: If a wealth advisor wants to sell me an annuity or some kind of complicated life insurance product, I bolt for the door. I will not pretend to be an expert on annuities, but I suggest that you Google their pros and cons before you ever consider buying one. As for complicated life insurance products: If you don't easily and fully understand the benefit of the proposed plan, move to the light. I own *no* life insurance in my retirement. My estate isn't large enough that I need it to cover inheritance taxes. My wife will have her own income stream that is sufficient for the lifestyle she wants when I die. For us, life insurance is not needed.

One more thing on life insurance. I am seeing a lot of plans that tell retirees they can get a minimum guaranteed investment income rate for life, and maybe more, and also be protected with life insurance. They sound so good. How can you possibly lose? Well, read up on the Internet, or ask your trusted banker or closest advisor to look at the deal. There seems to always be a catch, and it seems to never be in your favor. The devil is in the details.

Worse yet, several of my retired friends have been approached about buying life insurance, then were asked to sign it over to a stranger who collects when they die. They get paid a fee for their efforts. So let's think about this. Do you really want a stranger to have a financial interest in your dying? Sounds paranoid, maybe, but I am not ever letting the control of my financial instruments out of my own hands. I do not trust strangers, and neither should you. Scammers are everywhere. By the way, the paperwork involved in this type of life insurance policy usually includes such information as your Social Security number and other important personal facts. Do you want that out there?

Scammers target you when you hit a certain age or retire. Even if you are a smart guy or gal, they can trip you up. They got to my dad, and he was one of the smartest guys I've ever known. They have fooled me a few times, but I was lucky enough to catch the problem and take measures to protect myself before I had a loss. Just because you are really smart or really wise does not mean you cannot be taken. Be careful out there. End of rant.

BACK TO THE PLANNING.

You will have income from Social Security (and possibly some for your spouse), money from a pension plan or two, some cash saved to earn interest and to spend until you are legally required to start pulling out at least an annual 5 percent of your IRA balance, and possibly other funds from rental properties, bonds, and the like. If the amount you calculate adds up to what you figure you will need in retirement, great. You are financially ready to retire. If it does not add up, you have some choices.

Work longer until you have enough saved to provide the retirement income you require.

Simplify your retirement plans so you can live on less money than you originally calculated.

Re-calculate your retirement plan to do things like drawing down on assets to replace income streams that are short or missing. Of course, you need to realize that will increase your danger of running short on money in the future, and may leave you unable to pass along some of your assets to your kids or to charity.

If all of the above ideas still leave you well short of what you want for retirement, and you are single, marry someone who is financially secure. I am not kidding. That person will not find you. You must make it happen. And with any luck at all, you will find someone you like, who likes you, and with whom you can enjoy a financially secure retirement.

Step Eight: When Steps One through Eight are complete, when you are old enough to trigger certain benefits such as Social Security or your own company's retirement plan, take the plunge. If you do have a way to earn a bit of income in retirement working two days a week or whatever, all the better (at least financially).

A couple of footnotes to everything above. When I calculate how much income I can get from an amount of cash such as a lump-sum payment from a pension plan, I use 5 percent. Any professional retirement planner reading that number will have a heart attack. In today's economy, it is way too high. As I write this in 2015, "safe" investments earn about 2 percent or less. But doing some simple math, I use 5 percent as a rule of thumb, figuring that is probably a good number over time and is easy to calculate. Just know that it is a very optimistic number right now, and if you want to be safe, you should really be using a number like 2 percent.

IT PAYS TO BE CONSERVATIVE WITH YOUR ESTIMATES

A $1 million lump-sum pension payment earning 5 percent a year will provide you with $50,000 of income before taxes. That same sum times 2 percent will earn you only $20,000. You can see why a retirement professional would have that attack. I guess I would say that if you want to use the 5 percent for figuring things quickly and in your head, do so. If you want to figure things accurately so you can actually make plans based on the figure, choose something more conservative, like 2 percent or whatever the prevailing interest rates are at the time of your calculation.

AND BE CONSERVATIVE WITH YOUR INVESTMENTS

I want to point out a very important concept. You really cannot afford to put your retirement savings in high-risk or volatile investment vehicles. Once you have retired or gotten above a certain age like 55, your portfolio will not have the time and ability to recover from a catastrophic investment loss. And trust me on this—those losses do happen periodically, usually when you can least afford them.

I had this exchange with a buddy of mine recently. He had just shown me his list of investments, each one "iffy." You've never heard of any one of these companies, and each one pays a ridiculously high dividend. Some others toward the bottom of the list were penny stocks. I asked, "Why are you taking such risks on these fly-by-night stocks?" He replied, "Not all of us did as well as you in planning for our retirements, so we have some catching up to do. So I asked a high-flyer buddy of mine for some tips." Scary thinking. Scary situation.

Trying to hit that home run is almost never a good investment strategy. It is a desperation move. It is much more likely to screw you further into the turf than it is to get you wealthy overnight. There is always a reason for high rewards, and that reason is almost always high risk. My friend is just plain gambling with his retirement finances. I gave him my best advice. I hope he takes it.

One good rule that everyone can follow: diversify. Don't put all your eggs in one basket. Put some money in bonds. Some in real estate. Some in stocks. Some in mutual funds. Some in gold or other precious metals. I try to not have more than 5 percent of my assets in any one category. Study up on diversification. It will be time well spent. You may think you are exposed to losses in the financial sector only from the one bank stock you own. But what investments are lurking in that mutual fund you own? If you look carefully, it could be more bank stock.

Spread your investment risk. Take reasonable risks. Avoid high risks. Remember that high returns often mean big risks. What goes up comes down. Find a safe way to put your money to work for you.

"Invest in the future because that is where you are going to spend the rest of your life."

Habeeb Akande

CHAPTER TWELVE

WHAT IF THE NEST EGG LOOKS MORE LIKE AN EMPTY NEST?

"You might be a redneck if your retirement plans call for you living in your car for more than two years at a time."

Unknown

First, no judgments here. Life throws things at all of us that could easily lead to difficult situations down the road. If you are now down that road and coming up on retirement, really want or need to quit, and find yourself without much in the way of assets or income streams, well, this chapter may be of some help to you. If you are set financially, skip ahead to the next chapter.

The following ideas are a dozen mix-and-match sets of actions that can help you stretch your finances in retirement, or just plain get by.

First things first. Be honest with yourself and with your closest relatives about your situation. Put the cards on the table. Quantify your situation in real numbers.

One of the things I've encountered repeatedly is that the husband has not made the wife completely aware of their financial situation (it could easily be the opposite way around if the wife handles the finances and/or is the dominant breadwinner in the family). You cannot solve problems or get help with them if your fear or embarrassment hides the truth from others.

Second, it is what it is. If you need to have an emotional breakdown because the truth is out and staring you in the face, go ahead and do so, and see if you can be finished by noon today. If you are going to have a big fight in the family because you have come up on retirement, and now everyone knows that you did not do a great job of financial planning, saving, or investing, have that battle and see if it, too, can be finished off by noon.

It is what it is. Look at the truth of it, and get on with figuring out what you are going to do.

I'm not trying to pander to you with this next statement. It would be easier to ensure your retirement happiness with adequate money put away for that purpose. But I see people every single day of my life, usually at the beach, who are well into their retirement, who I am quite sure have very little more than their Social Security income or state welfare to live on, and they are some of the happiest people I know. *You* decide your happiness, not your bank account.

I'm going to cover a lot of ground here. Some will be of interest to you. Some of it won't. However, as I said, solving the retirement income problem is a mix-and-match solution, and here are the pieces.

If possible, work a few more years, and save as much as you can. Every year you continue to work will be highly valuable in resolving your issue. However, you have to remember why you are working "overtime"—to save for retirement. So cut your spending to the bare minimum, and put your money away.

If you need to, retire, and work a couple of days a week. The only problem with working a couple of days a week is that those kinds of jobs usually pay minimum or low wages. Much better to just keep working full-time for a year or two than doing it a couple of days a week until you are 80.

Downsize before you retire. This is just part of an overall strategy to cut expenses. Once I put my head around the concept of cutting my own expenses, I was amazed at how much I could save a year. I quit taking the newspaper, and now get my news much faster off the Internet. I got rid of magazine subscriptions, quit just about everything that drew down money monthly or annually, cut back on my insurance to cover only those bad events that might ruin me, stopped buying new stuff for a while, cashed out my life insurance, and on and on. I made a project of it and could not believe how much money I was able to save. It was almost fun. Almost.

Look into government assistance. I know, you've never taken a penny of "charity" or public money, and you don't want to start now. Pshaw! You paid into these plans for decades. It may now be your turn to reap some benefits. You don't ask, you don't get. You don't investigate. You don't even know whom to ask. Check it out.

Sell stuff you don't use. Get to know how Craig's List and eBay work, and get rid of the stuff you don't use that can generate some serious cash for you. Seriously: Will you really be using that silver service for 12 during your retirement?

Do it yourself. If you have the time, you can do a lot of things yourself, like painting the house or mowing the lawn. If you are retired and hurting for income, cut your expenses by doing things yourself. I hate this one, but it could come in real handy.

Move. If the cost of living is high where you live now, move to a cheaper place. I think Linda and I moved a dozen or more times during our married life. We found we could live almost anywhere if we had to. Every place has its good and bad points. Just pick a spot that seems safe and that features "cheap" as one of its good points, and move.

Look for places to live that are "senior-friendly." Some states have much lower real estate taxes for seniors or other such breaks. Hawaii, for example, has great real estate tax rates for seniors over a certain age (I think it is 60) who live here full time. My real estate taxes are about 20 percent of what they were in Illinois. Our sales tax is currently around 4 percent, compared to that in Illinois of 10 percent or more. Look carefully to see where you can save real money on your taxes. By the way, Hawaii's income taxes are relatively high, but most of us are not making a lot of money in retirement, so who cares?

Look for other senior discounts. They are all over the place. I am happy to show them my license to prove I am over 65 (like anyone has ever asked. I look like a salmon that has swum well upstream). One of the best ones is the pass you can get for our national parks. I think it costs $10 for a lifetime of admission to all of them. Heck of a perk for getting old.

Now a couple of big money items.

Rent rather than own. So far, I don't think I have ever been able to talk anyone into this one, but it can be a huge win. I will cover it fully in the very next chapter. Renting rather than owning can make your retirement financially possible.

Pay off high interest first. I know I have said this, but it is worth repeating. A great investment of any money that might come your way is to pay off your high-interest loans right now. I am talking about credit cards, car loans, and the like. If you have $10,000 coming your way and have to choose between spending it (can't do that right now, because you are trying to catch up on building your financial nest egg for your retirement), investing it (not a great idea, because anything safe these days pays about 2.5 percent or less per year, and you cannot afford to gamble for the higher returns), or paying down your Visa card that charges you an annual 14.9 percent—no brainer. Pay down the credit cards. Get rid of debt as the very foundation of your retirement financial plan.

Avoid the scammers. Listen carefully to this one, please. I know you are smart. You may be a seasoned business professional. But retirement finances are obviously not your strong suit, or you wouldn't be so far into this chapter. I see virtually everyone who reaches retirement age as the target of some kind of financial scam. It often works, because people are desperate.

I am so sorry to say that I see a lot of these scams originating through church contacts. Whoops! Pissed off a lot of people with that one. Just reporting what I've experienced. There seems to always be one really nice guy or couple in the church who is probably there to get money out of people like you. Watch out for them. They bury their financial poison in friendship and sheep's clothing. Just stay alert.

People who say they can get you 10 percent or more in the way of investment income are not being honest about the risk involved, or are just straight-up scamming you.

Here is one of my favorite scams that ran through a country club I belonged to, and it also showed up at a place where I worked. It went like this.

A guy everyone knew as very wealthy lets you in on "the chance of a lifetime." You can get in on the ground floor, and earn some serious cash. Guaranteed. You give him $1,000, and he pays you back $100 a month, every month, for one year, at which time, you get back your original $1,000. Since the deal is so good, the length of time to be out the cash is so small, and the rich guy is guaranteeing it, dozens of my friends signed up for it. It was also very tax-efficient—as in, nothing gets reported to the IRS. Wow. What a deal.

I did not participate in the deal and, when every single one of my friends who invested got paid off exactly as promised, I was made fun of repeatedly for being such a fool.

As soon as the first $1,000 got paid off, the deal had grown. It was now $10,000 for the next year. Every one of the investors signed on, and a few more friends, as well. Every one of those people got paid off exactly as promised. More gloating. More parties. This had become a big deal.

I think what bothered me the most was the lack of thinking on the part of the investors. Assuming this was a legitimate deal, how exactly were they going to earn that kind of money legally or morally? I have the same problem with people who invest in pyramid schemes. They have to realize that the only way they will profit is when those below them on the pyramid lose. That never seems to bother them.

The only way the above scheme could work would be if the rich guy were putting money out on the street at outrageous interest terms, or financing a dope ring, or something else just as illegal and/or risky. Traditional investments are highly unlikely to pay that kind of money. So here are my highly moral friends, some of them pillars in the community, involved in their church or other religious institution, otherwise good and solid citizens, willing to invest in a scheme they know nothing about. It could involve murder for hire for all they know. And they're willing to cheat the government (and the citizens of that government—you and me) out of taxes owed. What? I just never understood it. I think it is covered under the word "greed."

The deal got even better for these investors. In just a few years, it grew so popular that our rich-guy friend had to fence it in a bit to keep it manageable. From now on, he accepted only investments of $250,000 or more. That cut some of the earlier investors out of the deal, but most stayed in and put up $250,000 to $1 million. Our rich-guy friend would not take investments of more than $1 million, because he wanted as many people as possible to be able to participate.

After the round of high-stakes investing was done, things got very quiet. Rich-guy never showed up at club events. The first monthly payments were missed. The investors couldn't get in touch with rich-guy. His phone message said he was on an extended vacation and out of the country. Yes, he is, to this day. Everyone lost everything.

Well, the investors decided to go to the police, that is, until one of them figured out that they had not been paying taxes and would be confessing to a crime. They ate the loss. Some of those folks will be reading this chapter (but probably not this story) as their nest eggs go bye-bye with rich-guy. Sucks.

I don't care who you are or how smart you are. The scammers are after you. Be extremely careful. If something seems too good to be true, it always is.

One rule of thumb I have always used: I never do business with people who are financially smarter than I am. In other words, if they are dealing in products that are so complex that I can't understand them, I don't even try. I do *not* trust them to understand it for me. I've seen one of my employers nearly go bankrupt after hiring "the smart guys" to sell derivative products of the kind that got AIG and others in trouble in about 2008. Not a month goes by without one of my friends calling me for help in understanding "this deal that a guy at the club just offered me." I send each one running in the other direction.

At this point in your life, your investments need to be conservative, not wildly speculative. Anyone who offers you these high-reward investments fails to mention the great risk. Be careful, very careful. It is too late to re-build the war chest.

Always ask yourself before doing any speculative investment when the payback will come. If it is 30 years out, it's not a good investment vehicle for your retirement. Ask how you will earn money from the investment. Will it be cash, more shares of the venture, or tax credits? If it is tax credits, will you have a high-enough income to take advantage of them? What are the risks, what exactly are you investing in, how does it earn income, and how can you hedge your bet (for example, with a stop-loss order)? By the way, when the market dropped so fast in 2008, the amount I got for stuff I sold due to my stop-loss orders was way under the percentage I had placed because, below that point, the prices just fell like bricks. If you are not a lifelong investor, get a world-class wealth advisor (who will charge you quite a bit to manage your money), or invest in simple products like mutual funds that span the entire stock or bond markets.

And now, back to another strategy. Learn to use what is yours for free: the beaches, lakes, rivers, hiking trails, roads, campgrounds, libraries, public events, and the like. Some of this will depend on where you live, but I swear, I could spend the next year of my life paying nothing at all except for the gas to get there, using what is available to me in Hawaii, and still have a great life. Spending the next 365 days at a place like Kua Bay would work out just about perfectly and cost me nothing. I wasn't trained to live like that, but I could sure learn in a hurry. Your retirement happiness is not hardwired to your bank account. There is plenty of free stuff out there for you to do. Enjoy it.

Come to think of it, most of the clothes I bought at Nordstrom ended up lightly used, then went to a thrift store like Goodwill or the Salvation Army. I'm guessing my stuff joined the things from a lot of other people who were downsizing. Again, thrift stores would not be my first choice for shopping in retirement, but I would utilize them if I needed to. God bless those who run them.

I don't have many brilliant things to say about healthcare in retirement. As I write this book, too much is changing in our healthcare systems and options for me to be definitive. However, I will say this: Healthcare costs can be huge. The decisions you make about your healthcare can greatly affect how much money you have to spend elsewhere. I am in the process of switching over my healthcare coverage that sits on top of my Medicare from a corporate-retiree medical plan, which has been costing my wife and me more than $600 a month with huge deductibles, and which very few doctors on this island accept, to the most popular local HMO. It has new facilities, and for just $80 a month and low deductibles, it takes care of most everything, or will pay for your flight to specialists. Why did I wait so long? I was lazy and assumed that my corporate coverage had to be superior. When I checked it out myself, not so much.

So if finances are tight, work a bit longer, maybe take on a part-time job, cut your expenses, avoid the scammers, be conservative with what money you have, and see what is out there that you can tap into for financial assistance or use for free. Life is good.

"Creativity in retirement is knowing how to spend time without spending money."

Unknown

CHAPTER THIRTEEN

RENT OR OWN?

"Money can't buy happiness. But it sure can rent it for a while."

Kim Gruenenfelder

The subject I wrote about in my previous book, *The Way Up*, that caused the most hate and dissention was moving for the purpose of working your way up the ladder. I am in favor of moving if you need to, so that you might expand your options for success. Some readers were angry that I even brought up the subject. They couldn't possibly move, and how dare I give them that advice.

The topic in this book that will garner the same reaction will be this: **Consider renting a home, rather than buying or continuing to own one.** Hate me if you will for even bringing this up, but please take a look at my logic first. Here goes.

A home is a costly asset to buy and maintain. It may also be a storeroom for a large portion of your wealth. A couple of thoughts.

If you have all the money you will ever need in retirement, and your home is 100 percent paid for, it may be a great idea to continue to own it. In fact, it will provide you with fairly easy access to cash, should you need it down the road. All you have to do is get a mortgage or a line of credit backed by the equity in your house. Or you can get a reverse mortgage. You can extract a significant amount of the equity of the house you own.

If you own a home and do not have enough sources of income to live the way you want in retirement, you can borrow money on the house, or sell it and downsize, or rent.

If you downsize, you can use the difference in the money you got for your last house and the price you paid for your new one to subsidize your retirement lifestyle. For example, if you sold a house on which you owed no money for a net of $500,000 and bought a new, downsized one for $250,000, you now have a quarter of a million dollars in cash to support your lifestyle. If you put the money in a safe investment that earns something like 3 percent, then from it draw down $10,000 a year, you have that much extra annually to support your retirement lifestyle. You will be able to do that for the next 30 years or so.

If you take the whole $500,000 and invest it safely at 3 percent, it would earn about $15,000 a year, less taxes. You'd earn less as the original principle is drawn down. With the help of an interest table or an accountant, you could figure out a reasonable balance of what you might want to spend each month in rent, how much to draw out to support your lifestyle, and the length of time the money will last. It should last decades.

If you borrow money on your house or sell it, and use a bunch of the proceeds to buy a big boat or a fancy car, then head to the casino for some fun, things are not going to go well. Start researching how to get the government cheese.

I'm not sure why people are so attached to their homes. I guess it is security. Some of it may be a well-founded fear of not having easy access to all that cash. Whatever. All I am saying is:

think it through. You sure don't want to still be paying a mortgage in retirement. You certainly don't want to start a new mortgage once you are retired. If you are holding onto the home as an investment, who's it for? Real estate is not always a great investment. These days, property values seem to go up and down, says Don, who just sold his house for about 40 percent of its one-time worth, and bought another for about half of its original cost.

Renters sometimes get great deals. I have a close friend who just rented a house that I figure is worth $600,000. It is fully furnished. Has all the bells and whistles. The owner pays all utilities and taxes, including great cable and Internet. My buddy pays $1,500 a month. He could not afford to own this home right now. However, in renting, he is missing out on four things:

- Building up equity in the house. I advised him to put $250 a month into an investment account. He will be way ahead of the equity curve.

- The tax write-off. Do the math on this one. Say you pay $10,000 in interest on your mortgage, and you get to write off that full amount on your income tax. If your income tax marginal rate is 35 percent, you save an annual $3,500. If you do not pay $10,000 a year in interest and have no tax write-off, how much do you save? You save the whole $10,000. Ten thousand dollars is better than $3,500. So much for the I-need-the-tax-write-off argument.

- Missing out on the price appreciation of the house, which has averaged zero in our area over the past five years. Over time, most homes do appreciate, but there is also the trade-off against the price of needed repairs and maintenance.

- Missing out on paying the taxes, utilities, maintenance, insurance premiums, and those occasional horrible surprise bills:

the new roof, the water heaters, the leak in the basement or around the windowsills that rotted the wood. You know. The big, bad bills that come when you can least afford them.

So there is no perfect answer. However, figuring this out needs a full, open mind, and a pencil and paper in hand. If you are short on income for your retirement, think twice or more about your housing choices. Where and how you live can give you more income to support the lifestyle you want, or lock you into one you cannot afford. I have a friend who has a nice house, but cannot afford to pay his insurance and is always behind on his taxes. His cars are falling apart. He has to rely on the help of others to repair or maintain everything in the house. And with the cars, he has no money for that kind of stuff. He has already maxed out what he can borrow under a reverse mortgage. My prediction: It is all downhill from here. Will he sell his home and move to a place where he can afford to live? It's not going to happen. He has to own a home. I wish him well.

"It's easy to underestimate the real cost of home ownership."
Suze Orman

CHAPTER FOURTEEN

TIMESHARE OWNERSHIP: NATURE'S WAY OF SAYING YOU DID NOT PAY ATTENTION IN MATH CLASS

*"In school, my favorite subject was math.
That's where I learned to count money."*

French Montana

If you currently own a timeshare, congratulations, and I hope you take full advantage of it for years to come. This chapter is not for you. Move right along to the next chapter, please.

Smart people own timeshares. Rich people own timeshares. Lots of people own timeshares. Some of those timeshares have provided great getaways and vacations for whole families for decades. I am not against timeshares in any way except for the cost. And lots of retirees look at timeshares to solve part of their questions about where to live.

I looked at a timeshare opportunity recently. The facilities were *spectacular.* Anyone reading this book would be over-joyed to stay at this place—great location, facility, and rooms, and many fabulous perks and options. The one-time cost to us was $40,000 for a week of timeshare per year (very high vs. the average nationwide cost of about $11,000 a week, but this was not a typical property). Man, if I could make financial sense of this, I wanted to buy. Wait—it got better. If I signed a contract today, they would knock off $8,000. I am a cautious guy and wanted to think it over for 48 hours. Nope. The $8,000 offer is on the table until 5 p.m. today. After that, full price. The pressure is on.

Now, I once had a wise boss, Ted Hull, who told me, "Never make an important decision where the band is playing loudly." I must say, the very professional sales person was a band playing loudly. So my wife and I did the best we could. We went into another room, pulled out the calculator, checked some stuff online, and did some ciphering, as they used to say on *The Beverly Hillbillies*. Here is the way I figured it.

If one week cost $32,000, then 52 weeks would cost $1,664,000. I had noted that similar units right next door sold as condominiums for less than $400,000.

I took the maintenance fee of $1,200 for the week and added some other miscellaneous annual charges, which brought that total to $1,400. Extended over 52 weeks, the extra charges for that unit would have come to $72,800. The condos next door had an association fee of about $800 a month, including the taxes on the unit, or $9,600 a year.

Oh, for sure, there are some other important pluses and minuses on both sides of this equation that I am not considering, but the down payment and the annual fees are enough for now.

So, my costs would equate to purchasing one fifty-second of an asset valued at $1,664,000, but really worth only about $400,000.

I would be paying association fees at the annual rate of $72,800 vs. the actual condo cost of those at $9,600 a year.

No wonder they like to sell them as timeshares instead of condos. They quadruple their money.

Oh, and I am 69 years of age. I would be paying on this timeshare, use it or not, until I am a feisty 99.

Also, they would have my $32,000 forevermore. Imagine what the net present value of that money would be over all the years.

I looked online, and found that you could buy the same time-share in the secondary market for a song and a dance. The asset was not going up. It went way down almost immediately.

And I was locked into the same facility every year (which means travel costs), unless I wanted to pay a fee to choose some other location. As well, not every room or week of the year was available to me. There were several layers of flexibility that you could buy. Without that, you kind of took what they had to offer or paid that extra money to land another location.

I showed the salesperson my math, and asked her to help me make some sense of it. She smiled, folded her papers, and stood up. I asked her one thing before she left. I said, "For such a first-class presentation and top-rate facility, why would you plug in such a high-pressure technique as giving us just a few hours to accept the discounted deal?" She said, and I quote, "Because exactly 100 percent of the people we used to let think about it overnight did not make the purchase."

Shouldn't that tell you everything you need to know about a timeshare?

Timeshares come up for conversation often among people who have retired or are about to. I'm hoping that the title of this chapter will ring in your ears as you sit down with the nice-look-ing young lady or man, after savoring the fabulous free lunch and the great champagne, after enjoying the past two days in your 80-percent-off hotel room because you promised to listen to the timeshare presentation, and right before the luau you will attend as their guest tonight. Timeshares are for those who failed grade-school math.

"An investment in knowledge pays the best interest."
Benjamin Franklin

CHAPTER FIFTEEN

GET YOUR LIFE IN ORDER
BEFORE YOU RETIRE

*"Opportunity doesn't make appointments,
you have to be ready when it arrives."*

Tim Fargo

Nothing is ever perfect, but let's talk about it for a moment. It would be perfect if you tackled these 10 things before you retire.

- You get a full physical, and address any issues discovered. Good to get this done while you are still employed, have some sick time or disability plan if you need it, are familiar with your medical policy, and have people around to support you. Once you are out the door, you are more or less on your own.

- Same for your dental work. Get 'er done.

- You have your will, a power of attorney for health and one for assets, burial instructions, trusts set up, and good legal/ accounting advice on how to handle the resources coming your way in retirement.

- You have your house paid off.

- You have gotten rid of anything that even looks like debt. This includes credit card debt, car payments, leases, maybe even country club memberships. Anything that is going to cost you significant money every single month. We kept our country club membership for a couple of years, but then got rid of it. Total savings of about $1,000 a month. Got rid of our dining club social memberships, as well.

- We started the process of not renewing our volunteer positions. In other words, when the time was right, we exited stage left, and did so quietly. We noted that none of the organizations had to fold after we left. When so moved, we sent them our support in the form of a check. They seemed to like that kind of support.

- As the offers started coming in for me to join this volunteer or company board, or take on a short-term project after I retired, I quit trying to keep those people interested in me, and told them directly that I was out of that kind business forever. That seemed to work.

- A couple of job offers arrived. One of them was so big that it would stand your hair on end if I gave you the details. One was a commitment for six years, and the other for four. One would add significant sums of money to my retirement war chest. The other would just plain make me rich. I turned them both down. I was done. Best decisions I've ever made.

- You will need to have a mindset about consulting, if that is something that might come your way. My retired friends who are still consultants don't really seem to have their freedom. One of my favorite examples: I invited a guy to go to the Master's Golf Tournament with me—my treat. He couldn't go. He was waiting to find out if he had landed a consulting gig that would start that week. I went to the Master's with another friend. My first friend stayed at home, waiting for the phone to ring, and it never did. Are you in or out? My thought is, the clock is ticking. If you think you would really value your total freedom, go for it. Don't put obstacles in the way.

And by the way, I get it. My friend may have needed that money, and had no choice but to continue his consultancy. Great. But maybe he should have stuck around one more year to build up that retirement savings, rather than hang around, waiting for the phone to ring, for five more years as a consultant. You get only so many years on this earth.

- And is there one more hill that you have always wanted to conquer during your full-time working career? If so, put off retirement, and go for it. None of us get every single thing we had hoped for in a career, but if you are close to something, give it your all before you say goodnight. You will be proud of yourself for trying for the rest of your life.

"Life is like a maze, you have to go through different things to get to where you want to be."

Unknown

CHAPTER SIXTEEN

DECLARE VICTORY

*"Once you hear the details of victory,
it is hard to distinguish it from a defeat."*

Jean-Paul Sartre

I never comment on the quotes in my books, but I am going to on this one. Why? Because it perfectly illustrates my point. You win when you say you do. Jean-Paul points out that victory and defeat have a lot in common, enough so that it may be hard to distinguish one from the other. I think that is true about our lives. I have friends who made it to the number-two spot in companies that employed 60,000 people, and retired feeling they were failures because they never got to the very top. What complete bullshit. We win when we say we do.

I wrote on this topic in another book. After the book came out, a buddy of mine called and said that the subject had struck a chord with him. He had been waiting for some magic moment when he would know that it was time to retire. He had accomplished everything he needed in the career phase of his life. He then realized that magic moment was his alone to choose. He declared victory and retired. He is happy with his career, and loves his new life. In fact, despite his piss-poor ability to play golf, he got a hole-in-one the other day. When he reads this paragraph, he will know who I am writing about, call me up to say that I should have used his name, and lie directly to me about the quality of his golf game.

My dad worked until he was 70. His only regret was that he didn't work longer. Wasn't it Colonel Sanders who got all of his fame and fortune after 65? People retire happily at age 35, and some never, ever stop, living and working right up until the closing bell. There is no magic age for your retirement. There is a magic mindset.

OWN YOUR RETIREMENT.
DECLARE VICTORY AND MOVE ON.

The magic mindset is to own your retirement, even if you are fired and standing out on the street with a box of your belongings in your hands at age 63. **If, after due thought and consideration, you decide that you are done, stop. Declare victory, and prepare to move into the next phase of your life.**

DON'T MAKE A MOVE BEFORE YOU HAVE
THE NEXT STEP COMPLETELY SECURED.

I do have one saying that should never be forgotten or ignored. It is: You should never let go of one ring until your hand is firmly on the next. If, indeed, you have a plan for your retirement, and the financial means to start enjoying that phase of your life today, then pull the string and retire. If, however, you are quitting because it is just too painful to get back up and go into the arena, even though you will now have to massively scale back your retirement, think again. You do *not* have your hand firmly on the next ring. You are just plain giving up. Pull yourself up again and have at it until you reach your important financial goals.

Successful retirees are happy with their lives. They look back on their careers as successes. They focus on the positive things that happened to them, and have declared victory.

Other people spend the rest of their days on earth all pissed off at the way they were treated at the end, upset that they never got the chances they felt they deserved, mad at most of the bosses they've ever had, irked at the companies or institutions that never really let them succeed and, for reasons that always escape me, are now pretty angry at the government, as well.

LIFE IS TOO SHORT TO CARRY FORWARD GRUDGES, HATRED, AND BAD FEELINGS.

One of my great friends in life was a professor who spent something like 40 years at one college. The college screwed him financially (at least, that is what he said, and I have no reason to not believe him) as he was retiring. I heard conflicting stories about this screwing, but believe it to be a relatively small amount of money. No matter. To my friend, it is the principle of the thing. Net result: He has had nothing to do with the institution that employed him for some 40 years, provided a paycheck every other week for all that time, and still supplies a pension to this day. He didn't show up when the college honored him for his years of service. He has written them off completely.

Here is what I have tried to tell my friend, and he won't listen. Stuff happens. We do get screwed every so often. However, it isn't worth being aggravated and alienated from an institution you loved for 40-some years, stewing about it until the day you die. Life is too damn short. Get over it. At least try to narrow down your anger to one specific person, and then just don't ever speak to him again. Don't hit the erase button on 40 years of your life. That is not winning. That is being a victim.

Honestly, very few of us get the gold watch, the big party, and the "little something extra" to send us on our way to a wonderful retirement after a long and universally agreed-upon successful career. Most of us get an inadequate briefing by human resources on what to expect, a booklet on the process, and a mass of confusion about how things like healthcare plans work going forward—a whole lot of important decisions thrown at us all at the same time that can make or break us financially in the future. We get a layer cake and cup of coffee in a side room with a bunch of people attending, because most like those things. And we get a quiet send-out through the back door after handing in our credit card, cell phone, company ID, and parking sticker.

HOW YOU FEEL ABOUT YOUR CAREER IS ENTIRELY UP TO YOU.

When you retire, how you feel about your past life, and how that is going to affect you for the rest of your days, is entirely up to you. A couple of things to remember.

The place you retired from paid you good money as long as you were there. It didn't sign up to be your best friend, or to see to it that you felt highly honored and well-treated every day of your life. It agreed to pay you for work you would do. End of story. Don't try to make it more than it was. Unless it owes you money, it is not indebted to you. Take away the money, and every good thought you can recall about the company or institution, and the people you enjoyed working with over the years. Leave every regret, slight, bad feeling, and unhappiness in your wastebasket as you leave for home on your last day there. You will be better off, by far.

Declare victory. No victory is perfect or entirely complete. Just declare it to be true. You get to retire and go on to do other things in your life. You know you did a bunch of good things in the old job. Pat yourself on the back even if no one else does. Tell people you did great and that you are proud of your career. Write a book or two and call yourself a success (I beat you to that one). Don't worry, be happy. There is no value whatsoever in pulling along a very heavy bag of remorse, anger, and frustration with you all the way to the grave. The choice is yours. Choose victory!

RETIRE ON YOUR TERMS.

And if you have any say in it, retire on your terms. If you want a little party to celebrate with your friends, arrange one. If you would really rather quietly slip out the door (like I did), do so. I mention that I slipped away, but let me tell you the truth. My very last days on the job were spent as part of a team, running an international leadership meeting. I took full advantage of that opportunity to do several things:

- I said goodbye to old friends, and told them of my plans and how to stay in contact with me.

- I thanked people.

- I kept myself very busy so I had no time for the emotions that might well have set in.

- I wrote myself into the script so that I could have one more day on stage in front of a group I cared for and admired. I wore a tux, even though I could have gotten away with just a sport coat. Why? Because I look really good in a tux, and that is how I wanted them to remember me.

- I set myself up to sit with our guest speakers, who happened to be British Prime Minister, Tony Blair, and his wife, Cherie Blair. Why? Because I could. On my last day at work, I decided to be a little selfish.

- I used my talent (such as it is) to envision and write a unique opening to the meeting that was animated professionally, and put to energizing music to show off our company's capabilities worldwide, using the idea of a Russian Matryoshka nesting doll to continually reveal new things about the people and abilities of our firm. It rocked. Even the Blairs loved it.

- I served on a team that was completely international, and made up of people I admire and appreciate from all around the world, and was headed by one of my heroes, Dick Kearns.

The meeting was nearly perfect. I had a ball. The day after it was over, I got on a 6 a.m. plane and flew home. I stopped by the office to drop off the credit card, company ID, parking sticker, and cell phone. I gathered up my box-o-crap of the few things I wanted to keep from my office; kissed my fabulous assistant, Mary Fall, goodbye; shed a tear or two; and then went home to grab my wife, and begin the process of jumping up and down to celebrate the accomplishment of yet another important goal in our lives—the end of my career and the beginning of retirement.

You get to frame up the end of your career any way you want. You can do it if your career ended in a lonely parking lot, waiting for your spouse to come get you as you stood there with your personal possessions from your office in a crummy-looking box that you hastily filled right after they fired you. You can do it if you are at the Ritz, being handed your new Rolex, and everyone in the room wants to get up and tell a story about what a great person you are, and how much you've meant to them in their lives. You can do it if you have just arrived home on the early flight out of Orlando, after saying goodbye to your old friends. No matter how you go out the door, you do it. *We all go out the door.* They will forget about you *much* sooner than you think. They will forget about how you left almost instantly. That just leaves you. Frame it up in your mind in such a way that it adds something happy and positive to your life from that day forward, and put aside the screwings, big and small. That doesn't mean you can't press them hard for any money they might owe you. You are not a sucker. Get the money and get lawyers if you need them, and put away any bitterness that could bubble up if you let it. Smile. Be thankful. Enjoy the rest of your life.

"I have fought the good fight. I have finished the race, and I have remained faithful. And now, the prize awaits me..."

2 Timothy 4:7

CHAPTER SEVENTEEN

LET HUMAN RESOURCES KNOW YOUR LEAVE DATE. WATCH YOUR LIFE START TO CHANGE IMMEDIATELY.

"It is time I stepped aside for a less experienced and less able man."

Professor Scott Elledge
on his retirement from Cornell

There is life after your career. Lots of life. Happy times. Cool things to do. But all of that is after you retire. Before that actual date, keep your head down and pound away.

DON'T LOOK FOR THE FINISH LINE, RUN THROUGH THE FINISH.

A huge mistake I see people making is looking too early for the finish line. You become what you think about. If you think about being done, even if you still have a long way to go, you are already finished.

Employers sense when people are looking for the finish line. They help them get there sooner than they expected. Happens all the time.

Let me write about age in the workplace for a moment. Ever hear that no one wants you after you turn 50? Well, that is partly true. However, those are important years for you. They may be the highest paid years of your career. **They are not to be just thrown away.** If you can continue to be hard-charging, stay in the moment, do the things that make great teammates win, and bring your experience and expertise to the table in such a way as to also honor the talent, energy, and skills of those less senior, you can stay employed right up until you either have to retire due to an age restriction, or until the day you *choose* to do so.

I have a friend who recently told everyone that he planned to retire in six months. He was wrong. He got to retire almost the next day. Coincidence? I doubt it. Employers don't like keeping people on the payroll that they, right or wrong, think are looking to the finish line. They like people who have a lot more skin in the game, and are still giving their all to both survive and thrive.

My dad "retired" twice. The first time he retired was on a Friday. He was working on an airplane called the B-1 bomber and had been with the company making it for something like 37 years. He called me on that Friday and told me he was retiring. Quite a surprise to me and to everyone. I asked him what he was going to do in retirement. "Work!" he said.

The following Monday, he went to work for a company he couldn't name, at a location he couldn't reveal, on a project he couldn't specify. My dad went to work on the B-2—the stealth bomber. He stayed there for 10 years until a Friday, when he called me up and told me he was retiring. I asked him what he had been working on all these years. He told me to watch the evening news. That night, I watched the coverage of the rollout of the B-2 stealth bomber. Dad had run all the way through the finish line.

The finish line comes up soon enough. Plan for it. Expect it. Don't, however, mark it on the calendar and announce it to the world. You and your employer will be much happier if you do like my dad: Run hard, cross the line, and quietly disappear from the workplace.

"There is life after retirement, and it is better.

Catherine Pulsifer

CHAPTER EIGHTEEN

FREE AT LAST

"The reward of a thing well done is having done it."

Ralph Waldo Emerson

By the time I was ready to retire, I had experienced every fine thing in life that I'd ever dreamed of, except one. I had never had my freedom. When I was a kid, my parents ran my life (or gave that a great attempt). Then along came teachers. I did what they said I should (most of the time). Next up, coaches. Coaches ran me around tracks and over hurdles until my knees bled, my back hurt, and one leg was actually one-half inch longer than the other. After the coaches, the bosses—40 years' worth of bosses. From age 1 day to age 61, I was always at the beck and call of someone. Always accountable to someone. Always living on the timetable of someone other than myself. Not mad about it. It is just the way it works.

FREEDOM. UNIMAGINABLY GOOD.
AND WORTH ALL THE WORK.

And then—free at last. Free to have the writing career I had always wanted (this is my fourth book, and the third I've written since I retired). Free to spend time with the grandkids, on the golf course, and sitting in front of my big-screen TV, God, I love it. Free to see the world and able to spend more than one day at a time in each location. Retirement completely rocks.

"Happiness lies in the joy of achievement and the thrill of creative effort."

Franklin D. Roosevelt

CHAPTER NINETEEN

OUT THE DOOR AND ON YOUR WAY

"It is so hard to leave—until you leave.
And then it is the easiest damn thing in the world."

John Green

I doubt that you need much prepping for the actual leaving part of retirement. The one thing I might say is that it can be really emotional for some people. It can hit at that little part of you that knows who you are and what you do in this world, and make you feel a bit vulnerable and out of sorts. If you are having trouble dealing with the emotions of it, for goodness' sake, go talk to a professional. As Tupac used to say, "Life goes on," and I wish he could say that today.

"When words leave off, music begins."

Heinrich Heine

CHAPTER TWENTY

THE "SORBET" MONTH

"May the dreams of your past become the reality of your future."

Unknown

I worked for over 40 years straight, without ever missing a paycheck. I had a mindset, a determination, and a set of habits that, for better or worse, were me. I was used to having my details taken care of by an assistant. I was used to being the boss. I was used to always having more work on my plate than any one person could ever finish. I was used to being important, at least in my own mind.

On June 1, 2008, much of the above changed dramatically. As of my retirement date, I was in charge of no one. I did not have to get up at 5 a.m. every single day of the week. If I wanted to fly somewhere, I had to arrange for the airline ticket (I'll bet my fabulous assistant, Mary Fall, is still chuckling about that little surprise in my life). I had no work on my plate, and damn few emails in my in-bin, and most of those contained offers to buy Viagra in Canada. Yikes. Life had literally changed overnight.

My first week of retirement, we had to go to the East Coast for a wedding. About six hours after arriving in Myrtle Beach, my wife and I got into the single worst argument of our 46-year married life together. We stopped speaking to each other. I think that lasted about three days. Dead silence for about three days. About that time, some jerk ran into my rental car, then told me he was a cop and that I would end up being responsible for the wreck. This was a really big, scary-looking guy of about 35 years of age. I went off like a skyrocket. I scared him so bad with my erratic behavior that he left the scene of the accident. My wife videoed the whole thing, so we had it all to show to the police. They quickly arrested the guy, and found out he had nothing to do with the police, and he most certainly was not a cop. He ended up paying for the damages and may have gone to jail. And so it goes. My first full week of retirement. You think maybe I had some pent-up emotions there?

Week number two went better, or as we say in Hawaii, "mo betta." We got on a plane, flew to Utah, rented a car, and proceeded to explore that beautiful state for a month. I'll bet I didn't get 20 real emails in that month, excluding ads and mass-forwarded stuff. No long list of people to call back each night. Peace. Quiet. Freedom. Wow. After a month of exploration, I began to understand that life would go on, that my wife and our new life together could be absolutely fabulous, and the freedom was well worth the wait.

We then went home for a month of twice-daily golf rounds, working on all the projects that I had put off forever, and getting ready for our next big adventure—a month in Australia.

We did the month in Australia, and found that life had continued at home without our needing to be there. We then got ready for our first six-month trip to Hawaii.

I call this time in our life our "sorbet" moment. It was a cleansing of the pallet that got us ready for real retirement. By the end of the six months in Hawaii, trust me, I was retired. And I loved it.

"This is a new year. A new beginning. And things will change."

Taylor Swift

CHAPTER TWENTY-ONE

MASTERING TWO NEW WORDS: "NAP" AND "NO"

"Being unable to say no can make you exhausted, stressed and irritable."

Aulic Rice

OK, the light went on for me, as it will for you. Life really does change after retirement. Want to test it out even further? There is this thing that was invented by babies a long time ago, something forbidden to you for most of the past 40 or 50 years. It is called the nap. You can put this nifty activity back into your bag of tricks. Get tired, head into the bedroom or any place quiet, shut out as much light and noise as you can, lie down, and go to sleep. Wake up an hour or two later, wondering for a moment who and where you are. Bingo. You have taken a nap. Repeat as needed.

Naps—one of the very best things about being retired. Refreshing, and now guilt-free.

But a much more important word for you now is "No." You really do have to learn how to say No.

To me, retirement is all about your freedom. Nothing screws up your freedom more than accepting new responsibilities. People know that you are vulnerable as you reach retirement and when you are first there. So they try to offload their set of responsibilities onto you. You're flattered. You have all this newfound time. You want be important. You want to stay involved. You say Yes. Beep. Wrong answer.

Try a year or two of saying No when you first retire. See if you end up happier than when you always said Yes. If you really miss being on committees, boards, and special projects, you will find that the opportunity to join them will never go away. But try it my way for a while. It will change your life and also let people know that you want it that way.

Shortly after I retired, I was offered a fabulous sum of money to run an important meeting for a guy I absolutely love. This was right up my alley. I did it all the time during my working career. Pretty much just three days of work with some planning to be done ahead of time. I asked the guy if it would involve me swimming with dolphins. He said, "Of course not. I plan to work your butt off for a few days and pay you way more money than you are worth for your efforts." I said, "No dolphins? No, thanks." He said something to me that was a physical impossibility and hung up. He later emailed me to say he hated me and wished he were old enough to do exactly what I was doing—living my dream.

If you want to see what freedom—the real thing—looks and feels like, you must learn to say No, and then go take a nap.

You've spent decades building up a set of habits that made you a success in your work life and in general. Now is a time to see if you can live another way, happier and with less stress. A more flexible way. An independent way. Your way, not someone else's. You have to build new muscles to make this happen. One of those muscles is that powerful word No.

Try it. You will like it.

By the way, if you never really give No a chance, your life will continue on much as you have known it for years, filled with deadlines, meeting dates, responsibilities, stress, work, and bosses.

It is hard to say No. Say it, anyway. No is the true path to your freedom.

One more thought on saying No. One of my biggest faults in corporate life was my inability to say No. I overbooked myself constantly, and paid a price for doing so. I was a go-getter, and we go-getters like to say Yes and round up as much responsibility as possible. So, go-getter (I am speaking directly to you): Be extra sensitive to this little chapter. This No thing is super important to your future freedom. Again, give it a try for a couple of years. Turn down everything. My bet is you will find that your freedom and accompanying happiness will go way up. Choose the things that free you up, simplify your life, and take things *off* your to-do list and calendar. Just say No!

> *"Let today mark a new beginning for you. Give yourself permission to say NO without feeling guilty, mean, or selfish. Anybody who gets upset and/or expects you to say YES all of the time clearly doesn't have your best interest at heart. Always remember: You have a right to say NO without having to explain yourself. Be at peace with your decisions."*
>
> Stephanie Lahart

CHAPTER TWENTY-TWO

DISCIPLINE. HAD IT, LOST IT, AND FINDING IT AGAIN.

"Discipline is the bridge between goals and accomplishment."

Jim Rohn

The one thing I know about myself is that I am a disciplined guy. I am on time, rarely forget appointments, work out every single day, never forget to take my vitamins, and regularly see the doctor and the dentist—you can count on me. Well, it turns out that a whole bunch of that discipline was because penalties were in place if I missed something. In business, unreliable people just don't make it very far along the successful career path. Also, you see great results from your disciplined efforts. There is a reward for you.

Things change a bunch when you retire. In no time at all, I had abandoned my beloved Rolex for a (God help me) rubber watch. When that watch fell apart, I did not replace it. Within months of retiring, I had no idea what day of the week it was. I wouldn't know the day of the week now if it were not for the cruise ship that comes into the harbor below our house every Wednesday. So now, when I am asked what day of the week it is,

I think, "Let's see. The ship was in two days ago. Must be Friday." As to what the actual date is today, I am pretty sure I could get it right, plus or minus five days.

I've run a dozen marathons, including the Pike's Peak Marathon, up and down a 14,110-foot mountain. I'm used to running two to 10 miles every day. And lifting. And stretching. I've done it for decades. I am in shape and always will be.

Then along came retirement. Throw in an operation or two. Throw in an injury or two. Throw in some heavy international travel. Throw in no one watching over me or anyone working out with me. Next thing you know, I am a gelatinous blob. What the heck happened?

As with a substance abuser, the first good thing that happens is the person recognizes there's a problem. That recognition happened to me when one of the sheets I hung over all the mirrors in the bathroom fell off. Oh, the humanity!

To tell the truth, both my wife and I are struggling right this moment with regaining our discipline. We've never been delusional about working out, or said, "Oh, I get plenty of exercise. I work in the garden." We know what real exercise looks like, and now we have to re-find the will to get back to it. We will. We are starting to make progress in that direction. I would give you a time by which we plan to have this totally back under control *if* I had a real good idea of what day it is right now.

And it is not just working out. I have a completed, fully edited book that I wrote, sitting in my closet, waiting for one last rewrite before sending it off to the publisher. It has been there two years. I kind of fell out of love with the book and fixing it will take a lot of work. And I would rather go swim with dolphins. In the old days, I would have set a goal/date to have that completed, and would have banged it out the door. Today—no deadline set, and no one around to remind me that I am approaching, or have passed, the due date that I haven't even determined. No penalty for not having completed the work. I think I will go for a swim.

I could go on and on, but that in itself would not be very disciplined. So let me get to the point. Just be aware that discipline as you know it will change when you retire. Some of that is good-to-great. No more deadlines, and no more mandatory things to do each day. But some of that is really bad. None of us can afford to get way out of shape before, or after, retirement. Some things have to be done on time, like taxes. I sent mine in this year in October—just couldn't get it done by April 15. Put that on your watch list when you retire. Watch out for losing a bunch of your discipline, and make sure you keep after those things that really are important.

I don't know how to wedge the next bit into this book, so I am just going to cram it in here, because it is slightly related to the topic, and it is a great story. We retired to Kailua-Kona, Hawaii. We live just below the tropical area where Kona coffee is grown on the side of the Hualalai Volcano. Our view is of the ocean and harbor in Kona. There are horses, cows, sheep, goats, turkeys, peacocks, owls, hawks, and wild pigs all around us. My neighbor shot a pig while he was sitting on his lanai the other night. I heard the shot, and five minutes later got a phone call inviting us over for dinner. Kailua pork was on the menu.

Things are different here than in any other place I have ever lived—slower and happier. When I first got here, I stood out like a sore thumb. I got up early, ran around doing things all day, and rushed from place to place. I tried to slow down and did, to some extent. Then one day, in the parking lot of Lowe's, an old hippie-looking couple, seated in their car, waved me down to speak. The old guy said, "We've been watching you. You run,

run, run, inside the store, in the parking lot, and all around town. Why you in such a hurry? You no live on the Mainland anymore. You live in paradise. Slow down. Look around. Enjoy your life."

I asked the guy to get out of his car. He said, "Hey, I don't want to fight you. I want to help you." I said, "I don't want to fight you, either. I want to hug you." Well, his wife also wanted in on that action. We all got out, enjoyed a group hug, and I told them I was trying to slow down, and thanked them for reminding me I had lots more of that to do. It is really hard to break old habits.

Balancing a new discipline where important things still get done on a regular and continuing basis, with a new lifestyle of less stress and hurry, is not the easiest thing to do that I have ever encountered. I'm trying. Hope you will as well.

The following quote doesn't really fit this chapter, but it is so great that I have to include it.

"Do not bite the bait of pleasure till you know there is no hook beneath it."

Thomas Jefferson

And while I am at it, here is a quote you will see nowhere else. I heard this bit of wisdom tonight when I mentioned to my wife that I planned to stay up all night to make some major progress on the first draft of this book. Her reply:

"I don't care. I have new tires."

Linda was ready for the next adventure. Good for her.

CHAPTER TWENTY-THREE

SIMPLIFY

"It is not the daily increase, but the daily decrease.
Hack away at the unessential."

Bruce Lee

I'm guessing that you and I share something in common. As our lives went along, they became more complex. More duties to perform. More places and events to attend. More stuff to care for and store. More.

My dad had warned me early on. "Son, watch out, or your possessions will own you."

As my career progressed, my possessions got bigger and more expensive, and required increased upkeep. Twice, we had 8,000-square-foot homes. One of those homes was on six acres of manicured lawn and landscaping. Our cars got bigger and more complex. We bought stuff until we had no more room for it. For a time, we even spent hundreds of dollars a month on a storage facility for our excess stuff. We had stuff.

Eleven years prior to retirement, I got transferred to Chicago again. It was our third time living there. By then, the light had gone on that bigger was not necessarily better. We were smart enough to downsize a bit. I wish we had downsized a lot.

One thing I can say looking back. None of my possessions or homes or cars ever made me happy. My friends and family, and Linda, and the things and events we got to attend or see, and whatever few accomplishments I had along the way—those were the things that made me happy. Simple things like love and adventure and friendship.

So we decided to get things as simple as possible in retirement. Still working on it. We decided on a new one-story house with basically no appliances to maintain. You do not need heating or air conditioning where we live. You can heat water and generate electricity using the power of the sun. We got a new four-wheel-drive Jeep and bought the extended warranty, because I intend to beat the hell out of that car, and I am making good progress in that direction. We put all our bills on autopay. We hired people to come in and do the hard work around the house: trim the trees, take care of the pool, and fix anything that breaks. We bought a simple and inexpensive barbecue, and throw it away when it gets dirty or rusty. And you thought *you* were lazy!

We have workout equipment in our house, so we don't have to travel to stay fit.

The hardest thing has been dealing with our possessions. We inherited a bunch of stuff—old papers, and photos, and some antiques that would not be useful at all in Hawaii, but were family heirlooms. We accumulated a bunch of papers, trophies, and plaques, tons of books and computer disks, and so on. We must have had 100,000 paper photos—some in albums and some loose. We also had the negatives. We had the kids' school papers, report cards, baby teeth, drawings, and uniforms. We had big and expensive collections: baseball cards, signed baseballs, rocks, stamps, coins, and the like. Closets full of collections. We had about every tool ever made in triplicate, and I knew how to use about three of them, one being a screwdriver. We had art, lots of art, much of it in very expensive frames. Lots of sports equipment, enough to fill a rec hall, including about six full sets of golf clubs, none of which seemed to work properly. An aside: I have always been so desperate to improve my game that I have bought every single golf gimmick ever created. When you see some guy on Sunday afternoon TV, pitching a new chipping iron that claws the ball out of sand, deep grass, or water up to a foot deep, and then back-spins it onto the green and to within an inch of the cup pretty much every single time, know that I own that club, the limited-edition one with the cool carrying case. And it is covered in dust (at least the cool carrying case is) and buried in the back of my garage, because for some unknown reason, the club never worked that way for me.

And we had clothes, like 50 white shirts, 30 suits, three or four tuxedos, a couple hundred pairs of shoes, heavy jackets and sweaters, weighty drawers and boxes of them, worth tens of thousands of dollars new. Used—several tens of dollars.

I mentioned earlier that we just plain got rid of stuff. Gave the kids first chance to claim any of it, and they did take a few things. We then offered our stuff up, free of charge, to our relatives. Then to our friends. Then we put stuff out for a garage sale. Then we gave it to various charities. Whatever was left, we took with us or threw away.

Unfortunately, Linda and I were just unable to pull the trigger on some of our useless stuff. We still have some. Stuff we paid big bucks for that is honestly now worth about nothing. Hard to throw that stuff away. Hard to throw away old photos and letters and the like. We are still working on it, and have made great progress, with more to go.

My advice—start sooner rather than later. Simplifying your life is not a one- or two-step activity. It is a mindset, and will probably take you years. Have at it.

Linda and I have lived through several situations where people we cared for did nothing to get rid of their accumulated stuff. A couple of those folks were low-end hoarders. They also did nothing to make things easy for those who would need to care for them or manage their estates. What a mess!

Age is a bitch. It sneaks up on you. In my dad's case, he intended to clean out the belongings accumulated over his 94 years of life. He started the project. Two things got in his way. He lived through the Depression, and couldn't bear to get rid of anything. My prized possessions from my dad's estate are about 50 pencils, each less than a half-inch long, sharpened and ready for use. That pretty much sums up my dad's view on not wasting anything. Then age jumped directly onto his shoulders overnight. One day, he could get up on that ladder, pull down a box, go through it, and throw a few things away. The next day, he was physically incapable of even getting up the ladder. He didn't want to, but he left me a real mess to sort out, and I am still at it.

Linda and I decided to not leave anyone a mess. We are still working almost every day on getting rid of stuff. We are highly organizing the stuff that we intend to keep, and storing it neatly. We have all our paperwork in order, along with careful instructions to help our son and daughter as they handle our estate, or when they try to help us out when we are fully geezered up (that shouldn't happen for several months yet). We sat down with them to go over everything. They know our finances, the team of professionals we utilize to keep us going, and where things are hidden or stored.

When we moved into our house in Hawaii, our terrific land-scape designer told us, "Learn to love the lava." He was right. Lava takes little maintenance, and you do not need to water or fertilize it very often. It is simple. Embrace simple. We, of course, ignored that advice, and now have a beautiful, expensive bunch of plants and trees that cost us time, effort, and money every single month. Learn to love the lava.

Keep it simple. More freedom.

"They think I'm simpleminded because I seem to be happy. Why shouldn't I be happy? I have everything I ever wanted and more. Maybe I am simpleminded. Maybe that's the key: simple."

Dolly Parton

CHAPTER TWENTY-FOUR

CLIMB THAT MOUNTAIN NOW.
TAKE THE RIVER CRUISE WHEN YOU ARE 80.

"Dream as if you'll live forever. Live as if you'll die today."

James Dean

One of our best retirement decisions was to frontload our retirement with the more adventurous things we wanted to do in life. In fact, our first month of retirement featured a canyoneering trip that led us to our first huge rappel: a big, scary descent down the side of a remote canyon with no one to belay it. (Well, we actually chickened out of that one because of the sheer terror of it, but we haven't shied away from much since then.)

One day, we ended up at the bottom of the stones and structures that make up the fantastic place called Machu Picchu. It is at something like 8,000 feet of altitude. To really explore it, one must climb endless stone blocks—not even stairs. It requires a lot of effort if you want to see it all. We wanted to see it all.

We stood at the bottom of Machu Picchu and both had the same thought—sure glad we didn't wait to 80 to try to see this place.

I've had a couple of nasty bouts with cancer, and a few very narrow misses from the Grim Reaper. I know for sure that time is limited. I can also see myself and my age-group friends around me (let's be kind here) not getting stronger and more energetic. If you have adventures you want to take, get going early on, like now. There is no waiting in retirement. Have at it.

Save the river cruise and the transcontinental railroad trips for 80 and beyond. Or, if you wish, do as we recently did. We went on a cruise where the average age on board was seven to eight days prior to death. Trust me. You can wait to do that trip. Go have some fun. There is more to see in life than another museum or cathedral. Get off the beaten track.

That leads me to a touchy subject: risk-taking. I made my living for 40 years by assessing risk, figuring out how to mitigate or avoid it, and completing the deal. I still use those skills today.

Quite frankly, Linda and I want to do some of the most dangerous things on earth at this stage of our lives, and we've already accomplished bunch of them. But we do not want to do them foolishly. We are not looking to get hurt or killed, but know that could happen doing anything in life. We stack the odds highly in our favor. We hire the best guides or security people. We study how danger presents itself, and how to deal with it. We practice staying calm in the face of adversity. We follow instructions. We gear up with the best possible equipment. And discuss ahead of time how we will warn and protect each other. We know our limits and do not exceed them. And then we jump in and explore things that are way outside our comfort zone.

I bring this up, because most people are unwilling, or unprepared, to ever explore anything outside their comfort zone. My personal feeling about such people is this: What life are they waiting for? Why limit yourself? Why not give things a try under the very best of safeguards and circumstances? Don't miss out on life because of your fears. Turn those fears into experiences, things you are proud of, that get your giblets going.

I have a dear friend who is afraid of a lot of stuff in life, and she would be the first to tell you that is true. She can't swim. She decided, with our help, to give snorkeling a try. Good for her. By the end of the week, she amazed me when I asked her, "Now, if we go around that corner just over there, we will find ourselves in crystal-clear water about 50 feet deep, and could run into any kind of big fish (I failed to mention the word shark). Want to give it a try?" She said, "Yes!" Impressive.

By the way, Linda and I often jump in with really big, and potentially dangerous, sharks here in Hawaii, in Mexico, the Caribbean, Australia, and Egypt. Did you know that more people are killed each year by vending machines than by sharks? That is why we are very careful when we are around vending machines.

I have my set-in-stone limits. I will not skydive until I am at least 75 years old. I am not about to screw up my best retirement years with an injury. We don't scuba dive, because we are both a bit too stupid about being careful, and we hate having to deal with a bunch of equipment, and anyway, the best photographic light is in the first 25 feet. I won't do any technical climbing. I'm not great with heights. If I can hike up it without ropes, count me in. If I have to gear up to make it to the top, see you back at base camp. I won't subject myself to sheer drop-offs. My days in double-overhead surf are over. I now break too easily.

But short of those few things, bring it on. Could I get hurt or killed? Certainly. That is not my goal, and I would not like it at all. But it does happen, and it would make a great story for the grandkids to tell. "Yup, my granddad was photographing crocodiles, nose-to-nose with them in the water in a remote part of Mexico. All they found was his camera housing. Let me show you this cool shot he got—last one on the photo card."

One of the things I found when my dad died was the brochure his employer gave him on retirement and his benefits. Every picture in it showed a group of seniors doing something passive: sitting on a dock, looking out at a sunset, leaning over the railing of a cruise ship. Screw those people. I'm going out with a bang. We don't have to live into the expectations that others have for us. Let's surprise a few folks. You know you are winning the risk-taking challenge when your friends and relatives start to council you and express their concern for your safety. Let them live their lives meekly and in fear. The rest of us can push out our boundaries and see what else life has to offer.

"Wake up and live.

Bob Marley

CHAPTER TWENTY-FIVE

NEW FRIENDS,
PLUS OLD FRIENDS TO THE END

"If a man does not make new acquaintances as he advances through life, he will soon find himself alone. A man should keep his friendships in constant repair."

Samuel Johnson

One of the things I noticed right away when I retired was that my friendships changed. There were many people I liked whom I was no longer around on a daily basis. In fairly short order, I figured out that life had gone on for them without me. And my true friends from my workplace and career, well, we figured out how to stay in good touch despite the massive change in my life and the small one in theirs. As much as I wanted to include them in my daily play times, they had actual jobs, so could not join me. But that is what weekends, holidays, and evenings are all about.

As for my really old friends from my youth, some of them were still working, and others had joined me in retirement. Either way, I intensified my efforts to stay in good touch with my really old friends. Each of those friends held a memory chip, if you will, of my life that only that person and I shared. I *always* have time for my really old friends. And as they are making no *new* old friends, I make a conscious decision to lose none of them to anything short of death. That takes an ability to forgive, forget, tune out, and talk. But I will be damned if I am ever going to lose an old friend. They really are part of who I am.

This next part I originally featured as its own chapter. But it just starts off sounding so negative that I decided to bury it a bit inside this chapter. That said, read this through, and give it some thought. For better or worse, it is how I actually think. It may disgust you, or you might just change the way you think about people. In the end, it is about saving relationships and friendships—my method for coping with some of the most difficult people-related issues in life. So here goes.

PEOPLE ARE A NEVER-ENDING SOURCE OF DISAPPOINTMENT

I've wanted to write this piece for years. What has held me back? A lack of confidence that I can articulate this concept in a way that conveys it as a positive outlook on life, rather than the jaded comment it appears on first reading. I think I found the confidence to make it work. You will be the judge, and I do have confidence in you!

I see people running out of friends. Yup, some of them die or just drift away. But I am writing about people who are running out of friends *on purpose*. They are actively writing them off, one after another. Why? Because their friend or relative did them wrong.

GIVEN TIME, WE ALL DISAPPOINT

"Did them wrong" is a powerful thing. It hurts, embarrasses, and does physical or emotional harm when it happens. The problem is, give us long enough, and we almost always seem to do someone wrong.

There are so many common wrongs. Passing a secret on to someone else, talking behind another person's back, choosing one friend over another for something special (like being the maid of honor). Stealing from you, not paying back money that is owed, not believing in you and raining on your dreams, dating the wrong person and hurting your friend in the process. Taking on new friends that the old ones don't like, betraying a trust, being disloyal—and the list goes on.

Two problems. One: Given long enough, we all do these things. Two: You only get so many "old" or best friends/parents/brothers/sisters/teammates.

EXPECTATIONS

I actually *expect* that, given enough time, every single person in my life will let me down in some important way. I think my wife will. My parents. My kids. My best friends. Even I will let myself down. I think it is a certainty.

That being the case (and I believe down to my bone marrow that it is true), and given that I want to hold onto unique, one-of-a-kind and/or important relationships, how am I going to keep from pulling out the grease pencil and just scratching these evil-doers off, one after another, until there are none?

It has happened to me and my beautiful wife.

My wife and I used to be very close friends with neighbors we had known for years. During the time we knew them, our kids grew up, our responsibilities at work expanded, and we did a lot together. We were very good friends. Over time, they became exceedingly wealthy. They began to buy things like second homes, and went to great lengths to share their newfound toys and events with us and the rest of the gang of old friends. They were so generous that it was kind of embarrassing. None of the rest of us had the financial means to reciprocate. Had I been in their shoes, I might have become a little irritated.

Oh, they became irritated. Out of nowhere, and without saying a single word to any of us, they just completely cut us out of their lives. That is the second time this has happened to me. The first was when my best friend divorced, and his ex never again made or allowed contact with me or my wife. In both cases, although I guess I can see why they might have done it, it hurt. I figure you get only so many old friends in life, and they are impossible to replace.

So here is my point. Don't be so surprised when you get stabbed in the back by someone you love. It happens. It is painful. It diminishes your ability to trust in the future. It sucks. However, if that person is unique to you and important in your life, you need to give it every effort to find a way to heal the relationship. The specter of that process is, in itself, so painful that it normally just doesn't happen. Something really bad comes. Feelings are hurt and hurt bad. Out comes the grease pencil. And away go the problems, down the drain. That person is out of your life.

You may have to be the big person here and, even if you are the wronged party, be 100 percent accountable for the relationship. Find a way, on your terms, to get the relationship back up to an acceptable level. I'll agree with you that it probably will never be what it once was (although it may get better over time), but if you can keep talking and find a way to let that person know how the actions impacted you, the relationship can be saved.

And consider this. If you give someone a present and expect to get one back in return, it is not really a gift. Giving someone the benefit of doing 100 percent of the work to restore an important relationship is a gift, any way you look at it. Give the gift.

THERE IS NO WAY TO REPLACE OLD FRIENDS. YOU MIGHT HAVE TO ACCEPT THEM, FLAWS AND ALL.

You get only so many old friends, and one set of fathers, mothers, sisters, and brothers. As much as you love and trust them, these people (and you) are a never-ending source of disappointment. That, unfortunately, is how life works. Be prepared for it. Deal with it. And be better for it in the long run.

OK, I've beaten that point into a fine powder. Moving on.

Once I retired, I found I had access to a whole new set of potential friends. I never even knew these people existed. Who knew that, if you went to a country club at noon on a Tuesday, there might be two dozen guys and gals there, having lunch together, playing golf or cards, or just sitting around "talking story," as we say in Hawaii? And it isn't just at some fancy country club. These days, it is at the beach. There is a whole crew of people there every single day, and I like almost all of them.

Liking almost all of them is an interesting development. In the old days, I am sorry to say that a lot of my relationships were formed after being sent through a filter. I didn't even realize it then, but I sure realize it now. Close to me during my working years, I had old friends and relatives, neighbors, and those in the community or at my job who were facing similar challenges: building our reputations, networking, taking on tasks together, or helping one another with the demands of our personal and professional lives.

Today, my filter is: *Can we have fun together?* I could care less what their station in life is, what they feel politically, their religion or race, or whom they sleep with. If we have found a way to have fun together, that is all I need to know. I'm not moving in with these folks. I'm doing stuff like surfing with them. This new openness has really brought a lot of happiness to my life. And by the way, since moving to Hawaii, I have not been asked even once what I used to do. My two best friends here actually laughed aloud when I told them one night that I had been the CEO of a sizable business, as if they didn't believe me.

Here is the strangest thing of all about new friends. They can open up opportunities for you that you never thought existed or ever dreamed of in your life. And you can do the same for them. I'll save that story for a later chapter about finding a *completely* new and lucrative, satisfying, enjoyable, easy career, when I wasn't even looking for one. More to come.

If I decide to send this draft to my great friend and editor, Bob Gorman, this next part is one of the passages that he will cover in red Sharpie and remind me that I have a tendency to pontificate, and that habit is really annoying. He will also remind me that I am being redundant, that I covered this point earlier in the chapter. No worries. Here is some more. Let me find my really fancy, pointy hat and put it on, and away we go.

This book is not about our mortality. We all grow old and die. Heck, some of us don't even get to grow old. This book is about planning for your retirement and really getting the most out of it, maybe even more than you might have envisioned before you read this. That said, I just feel obligated to bring up a really touchy subject: your relationships.

Virtually none of us get to retirement age without having something in our lives that we really regret, or relationships we feel bad about losing. Does "pretty much everyone" include you? Have you not spoken to your brother in about two years? Did you just give up on your college roommate the second time he went into rehab? Did that old boss you loved for two decades finally do something to embarrass you and you wrote him off forever? Did someone drop you like a hot potato and you did nothing about it?

Why do I bring this stuff up? The reason is that the clock is ticking. Now that you are retired and have the time to deal with relationship problems, I urge you to consider doing so. If that relationship problem has gone on this long, it is probably 100 percent up to you to attempt to heal it. That means you have to make the first move and contact that person. That means you may have to apologize for something you feel was at least 50 percent or more someone else's fault. That means you might even be rejected once again when you do make contact.

SOME RELATIONSHIPS ARE 100 PERCENT UP TO YOU

I was raised to meet people in the middle. You move a little, I do the same, and we will find a way to get along. What about that stubborn ass that won't move? Well, if the relationship is important, you may have to be the one that does all of the moving. That might be the *only* way to get the relationship back on solid ground.

If your mom stops talking to you, I want to submit that is a problem. You get only one mom. She may be a difficult person (happy to report that my mom is a completely non-difficult person, and I love her every day of my life). She may be so difficult that she has really made you mad and hurt. And she might play hardball, cut you off. Doesn't open your emails. Doesn't answer your phone calls. Doesn't want to see you over the holidays. As I said, a problem.

I'm here to say that having a breakdown with your mom or dad, or your brother or sister—that just can't stand. If it does, you will someday find yourself standing over their graves, telling them all the things you would have said to them in life, had they been willing to listen. Talking to the dirt. Dirt doesn't listen.

There is no room for a bad relationship with a mom, dad, sister, or brother. And if they won't meet you halfway, it is 100 percent up to you to get that relationship back on track. It is one of the hardest things in the world to do, and that is why so few people do it. You can do it.

Taking 100 percent responsibility for an important relationship will cause you to humble yourself, control your frustration and anger, and test your resolve to never accept No for an answer. It will cause you to keep trying when you want to give up. Not react when the other party doesn't play fair. It is one hard, son-of-a-bitch thing to do. But it must be done.

WHERE THERE IS COMMUNICATION, THERE IS STILL HOPE OF A GOOD OUTCOME.

The key to making any relationship work is to keep communicating. If that takes an apology from you when you feel it should actually come from the other party, do it, anyway. If that means humbling yourself and telling this angry person that you really value your relationship, and that you are prepared to do whatever it takes to restore it to a good place, go for it. When that person spits on your attempts and rejects you, keep going. If the relationship is an important one, it is 100 percent up to you to get it back to normal. The other person just does not have the skills to make this work easy on you. It is up to you.

Who in your life right now do you think is too difficult to get back into the "good-relationship" column? Once you have that list put together (and I hope it is a short one), what is your commitment to restoring those relationships? Too difficult? Too painful? Too bad. It is 100 percent up to you. Pick one out, and get to work. When you find that you are successful, you can add some more, and then use the techniques you've developed to nip these problems in the bud *before* you reach the let's-go-to-our-corners-and-stop-talking stage.

No bad relationships. A commitment, not a concept. And by the way, activating the commitment is often 100 percent up to you.

I'm not writing a book on relationship repair, and you can breath easy that I am almost at the end of this rant. But I am here to say that the ball is in your court, the clock is running down, and if you are ever going to try to fix something that is not right in your life, now is the time. End of sermon.

Oh, and by the way, I am reminded that I still have work to do in this area—serious work. The ball is in my court, as well. I wish us success in dealing with our challenges.

"Love your enemies in case your friends turn out to be a bunch of bastards."

R. A. Dickson

CHAPTER TWENTY-SIX

EXPLORE YOUR PASSIONS

"A writer writes. If you want to be a writer, write.
This concept can be universally applied."

Unknown

Did you ever wonder what happened to that kid in your eighth-grade class who was a fabulous artist? With Class-mates.com and Facebook, it is easy to find our old friends and get a glimpse into their current lives. Almost every time I take such a peek, I find virtually no mention of those early talents.

CREATIVITY GETS BURIED UNDER REALITY

My theory is that the weight of reality just plain crushes a lot of our creativity. You and I have such a hard time just making it through the week in our current jobs, we ignore that God-given gift of creativity that is still inside us, long forgotten and never developed.

Those who have the lives they want find time and create space for the creativity to re-emerge. They let it come out in small forms at first, fan those fires, and let it roar later on. In many cases, that early-identified creativity becomes a central force in their later lives. It becomes something that provides fun and a feeling of accomplishment, and that connects them with others who share or admire their talent.

I have a hero in life who has always seemed to embrace his own creativity. Remember the big meeting I mentioned in an earlier chapter, the meeting for our top leaders in the North American part of our country, 500 of them, I might add? Well, this gentleman, Dick Kearns, flew over from the home office in Switzerland to attend that meeting. He was our chief administrative officer at the time, and hard-wire connected to the overall CEO of the company. He came to rehearsals, as we had tipped him off to the fun to be had. He thought that we were putting together a unique and powerful meeting, and told me so. He also asked, "Don, could you carve out 15 minutes for me to sing on stage?" Say what? "You want to sing in front of this crowd?" I asked. "Yes," said Dick. "Well, Dick, I have no band, no soundtrack equipment, and no budget for such gear. The meeting is tomorrow, and there is no time for you to rehearse your band or backup singers." "No problem," said Dick. "I'll sing alone with no musical backup."

I almost fell to the floor. This wonderful, full-of-fun Irish American was going to risk making a fool out of himself to get up and entertain the crowd. And he was going to do it alone. What could I say? He was way up the food chain. I smiled and said, "We will make it happen for you."

We carved out a space. When the time came, he grabbed the microphone and started singing. First, who knew that he was a great singer? Also, who knew that he was really good at taking popular music and changing the words to fit the business situation? And finally, who knew that he was also a professional singer and could pull the whole thing off to the wild cheers of the crowd? Not me, I can assure you. I love people who have unexpected talents and share those gifts with the rest of us.

MY UNEXPECTED TALENT—PHOTOGRAPHY

I guess this is as good a spot as any for me to tell you what resulted when retirement created an opening for me to pursue one of my old passions—photography. What resulted was everything. It virtually *made* my retirement. Here is the story.

Linda and I never really talked much about what we would do in retirement. We spent a great deal of time talking and worrying about where we would retire. When we got around to our semi-magical conversation about what we really wanted to do and avoid in retirement, the possibilities for our new lives just opened up.

These are the three headline items we wanted: our freedom, being comfortable outdoors and in the ocean every day of the year, and traveling. A throw-away item, well down the list, was that we both wanted to re-connect with the areas of our lives where we felt we had some creativity. For me, that was photography. For Linda, that was her art.

But enough about her. Let's talk about me.

I have always been a photographer. I had a good eye for photography. I went to interesting places to photograph. I owned the good equipment. I knew next to nothing about the technical side of using a high-end camera. I had some really bad habits that kept me from getting some of the photos I was desperate for. I had zero view of ever being a professional-level photographer. Why would I do that? Too much work and too much competition. Even if I got good at the art of photography, what would I do with my images? Honestly, becoming a professional photographer never even crossed my mind. I just wanted to learn the art and enjoy grabbing a few great photos.

Within six months of retiring, we had been on two long trips where I lugged around my camera gear. The results of my efforts were OK, certainly not great, certainly not the kinds of shots I always admired in *National Geographic*. Kind of frustrating, really.

Then, on our first winter trip to Hawaii, things changed. We went on one of the most interesting adventures of our lives—a night trip in a small boat through heavy surf and heavy seas, in pitch-black darkness, out to where the lava was flowing into the ocean. The trip was terrifying going out. I think that everyone except Linda, the captain, and I were seasick. I could hear the guy in front of me praying the whole time.

When we reached the lava flow, shortly before dawn, the sea calmed down, and the scene was absolutely magical. I probably took 500 photos. We got so close to the lava flow that you could feel the heat, smell it, and hear it rushing into the ocean. An amazing thing, indeed.

The guy next to me said, "Man, there is nothing in the world I would rather be doing than this." I said, "I disagree. I would rather be one of those two guys standing up there on the cliff, right next to the lava flow." Sure enough, right there, unreasonably close to the lava, silhouettes in the dark, were two guys with cameras on tripods, getting up-close-and-personal photos of the flow.

The guy said, "Well, one of those two guys is my son." I was stunned. I asked him how to get in touch with his son, and he told me about a boat he worked on. The next day, Linda and I were on that boat. The next day after that, C. J. Kale, Nick Selway, Linda, and I were standing right on the spot I had hoped to visit. And be careful what you wish for. It was terrifying.

C. J. and Nick were already professional photographers. They had not yet done much to make a living out of their efforts, but they were winning contests, and selling their images from a kiosk at night, and to magazines, and as book covers. They didn't seem to know much about business, but holy cow, they could shoot.

Linda was using a point-and-shoot camera, and only mildly interested in photography. She was mostly along for the adventure. Trust me. Hiking out to the lava at 3 a.m. when it is two hours each way—that is an adventure. I, however, saw this as a much bigger opportunity for new friends (now that I was out of the corporate world, I was just a bit short on those younger than 60. I pegged C. J. and Nick as about 25 and 30). It was a chance to finally learn how to use a high-end camera, and a great way to tap into the knowledge and access those two had on the island of Hawaii. They knew where to go and how to get there.

Well, we started hanging out with C. J. and Nick, and our lives dramatically changed. All the things we always wanted to do, we were doing them. They were reliable, didn't seem to have a bunch of scary habits, and were honest and fun to be around. What they saw in us, I can only guess. I think they saw two people, maybe the only ones they knew, who could join them on an adventure at the drop of a hat. They certainly saw us as different. I think they also thought that we could help them think through their business plans. Over time, it turns out that we all got along well and enjoyed each other's company. This was a pretty big surprise to all of us. Linda and I were actually older than their parents.

It turns out that I am an awful student when it comes to how to really use a camera. My bad habits got in my way. I always shot on auto, never used a tripod, and opted for the easiest editing software known to mankind. I had the mistaken notion that the only good photo was the shot as it came out of the digital camera. Nothing really needed to be done with it in the way of an edit.

I was also just plain ignorant about the technical side of things. I had no idea that a camera with a small image sensor took photos that did not look so great if you tried to blow them up to a size someone might want to buy. They looked grainy, and I really couldn't figure out why. My little underwater camera fit fully inside my hand, took some good pictures, and missed a whole bunch of other ones, because it was slow to shoot when you hit the trigger, and the resulting photos just plain fell apart when I tried to blow them up. Pretty disappointing.

By now, Linda and I were risking our necks alongside C. J. and Nick on the lava, in the ocean, and in scary places here and there. An aside.

I was a pretty gutsy kid. I would go out in big surf. Climb mountains. Go places that made others hesitate. Somewhere along the line, I got cautious. By the time I retired, I was quite cautious. Turns out you can't be all that cautious around C. J. and Nick. They will just leave you in the dust, and you may never find your way home. A problem.

I found that my caution was causing me problems. As kids, we had to do the rock dance, jumping across a bunch of stones to get to the places we liked to surf. They were uneven, wet, and slippery, and jagged as hell. I skipped across them like they were flat pavement. Now, 50 years later, I no longer skipped. I crept across the lava rocks near the beach or out in the fields. Not only was I slow. I found that I was having a lot more accidents, or close calls, because of my extreme caution. It took a while, but I regained my confidence, and I am skipping again. Granted, I can't skip as long or fast as I used to, but I can get from point A to point B while still keeping C. J. and Nick in my field of view.

Over time, I also found that my caution was causing me to miss out on lots of the fun. I just had to overcome my fears if I were going to really get to see and do all I wanted. I'm not sure how C. J. and Nick put up with it, but over time, they got me comfortable with being back out in big surf, in the water with sharks circling around us, trying to take our heads off, in murky water before sunup (don't try that one at home), and walking on top of lava that had been running just 30 minutes earlier. They got me climbing down cliffs in the middle of the night with 30 pounds of camera gear on my back, and lava dripping just yards away, hanging off the side of a mountain to get a shot (I hate heights), and driving down roads designed for donkeys with a death wish. Now this one is just plain stupid. They got me hiking out in bear and wolf country at 3 a.m., with no weapons or safety equipment, without any idea where we were going or what we would find, with wolves making noise just off in the distance. There is no doubt that C. J. and Nick are unreasonable risk-takers. Me—not so much. But over time, I got my mojo back, and now I can try to get myself killed just like the guys. Linda is just a little behind us on the "go-for-it" deal, but she has crawled *way* out on the limb with us. And guess what. It has added more to our retirement than anything else. We feel alive, and energized, and nervous, and ebullient. We are not shrinking into the dust. We are creating dust. Can all this go tragically wrong? Oh, yes, it already has.

On one of our trips out to the lava flow, C. J. took one misstep. He looked up for just a moment, because he thought he saw some lights ahead—other people out on the lava field. He was three feet in front of me. I did not look up, because I was always scared to death out there, so my focus was riveted on my feet and the ground just ahead. Next thing I saw was C. J.'s shirt disappear in front of me! He had stepped into a crack in the old lava that was 20 to 25 feet deep. I fell to my knees, and when I did, my hands were on the edge of that crack. I looked down to see where C. J. had gone. He was crumpled up on the rocks, way down below. He looked dead. I thought for sure he was dead. So did Nick. Nick went into hyper-rescue mode, jumping all around the dangerous lava field, trying to figure out a way to get down to C. J. I had to calm Nick down. My fear was that he would take one wrong step and end up on top of C. J.

After a minute or so of us shouting at C. J., he awoke and looked up. He succinctly assessed his situation. C. J. said, and I quote, "I broke my fucking leg." Happier words, I had never heard. He was alive.

There was no way to get him out. No way to get help. C. J. was in a lot of pain, and maybe bleeding to death, for all we knew. We finally figured out that he was semi-OK, except for the compound fracture to his leg. We then informed him that if he wanted to get out, he was going to have to pretty much climb up on his own. Turns out that he wanted to get out. He managed to climb within about 10 feet from the top of the crack. We had him throw us his backpack, which we then used to just gorilla-pull him out of the hole. Of course, the sides of the crack are lava, basically fractured glass. We just shredded his underarm and chest area as we pulled him out. But he was out.

I've never seen anyone in as much pain as C. J. Nick was also soon to be in pain as he tore apart his $600 tripod and used it to form a splint for C. J.'s leg, which, at the ankle, bent into a 45-degree angle. I was elected to take the heavy camera gear and hike it all by myself back to the car. That did not go well. Fortunately, C. J. and Nick figured out that task would probably kill me (and they would lose their expensive camera gear). Out of the dark came Nick to the rescue. We split the cargo and made it back to the car while C. J. waited for us, alone and in pain. When we got to the car, we quickly found our medical kit and opened it. It had one aspirin and a Band-Aid. We hiked that emergency medical kit back out to C. J.

We tried carrying C. J., but that just didn't work. His leg was too sore to be handled. So Nick got on one side of him, I got on the other, and we "Weekend-at-Bernied" him across the lava field. C. J. is shorter than Nick and I, and for some reason, was babying the leg that had the bone sticking out. Net result—he basically hung on my and Nick's neck the whole way back. Screwed up my neck for a month, but it was worth it, because we made it back to the car. I'm guessing that the whole ordeal, from falling into the crack to getting back to the car, took maybe two hours. By then, C. J. was just a bit cranky. No problem. We set the GPS for the nearest hospital, and off we drove. The GPS delivered us to a dead end in the middle of a tropical rainforest and announced, "You have arrived at your destination." That even got a laugh out of C. J., who, by now, was laughing very little.

When we did get to the hospital, we stuck with C. J. right up to the point where the doctor said, "OK, let's see if we can get that bone to go back under the skin." At that, Nick and I ran out the door and headed to breakfast. Several hours later, we returned just as C. J. was rolling out of surgery. He woke up with me next to him, and the first thing he asked was, "Are we still going to Ruth's Chris for dinner tonight?" We were not.

So I'm not advocating that you start risking your life in retirement. But I do want to touch on risk-taking a bit more, and will do so in another chapter. C. J. is now fully recovered, and tells the story in a very different way than Nick or I do. You should trust our telling of it, not his.

Back to the camera. Maybe because of my advancing years, but more likely my flawed personality, I was not a good student of learning the technical side of photography. I fought doing things the right way for a very long time, and I have the bad images to prove it. Then, a couple of things happened. First, C. J. walked by me and noticed I was shooting in auto. He told me that if he ever caught me doing that again, he was going to shove the camera *and* tripod up my ass. I've had my ass for a long time, and was pretty sure that would be uncomfortable. So I started using the settings on the camera as they were intended. Same thing happened when I tried to shoot in low light without a tripod. That was the end of my no-tripod days. Next, C. J., Nick, and I stood side by side on the edge of an iconic river, just outside of Yellowstone National Park, cameras on tripods, waiting for the sun to rise just enough to light up the mountains and the fall foliage. We all had the exact same equipment. I made sure we all had the same settings (I had learned to quietly go over and peek at theirs when I was unsure of the right ones). We were all within five feet of one another. Their images from that morning were world-class. Mine were good, but nowhere near world-class. That's when I learned that I should have been listening when they taught me about filters.

One more thing happened. We got back to our hotel that night and had dinner. C. J. said, "Let's meet at the car at midnight." I asked why we would want to do such a dumb thing on a cold evening in late October. He said, "To photograph Old Faithful." Now, I knew there was no moon that night. None of us had brought any flash or lighting gear. But to my absolute astonishment, by 2 a.m., Nick and C. J. had taught me how to use long exposures to shoot in near-total darkness to get some of the most beautiful photos I've ever seen. By the end of the evening and that trip, I actually knew how to use a camera. Once I had crossed that line, I put together a portfolio of photos worthy of a professional, entered and won a couple of big contests, and began to think about how I could actually make a business out of this new talent. More on that later.

Linda and I explored several other areas where we could connect with our own creativity. She worked with clay. I did a bunch of writing. But pretty soon we both turned back to the camera. The camera gave us an opportunity to participate in some amazing adventures, travel around the world, and create some images that others turned out to enjoy. We were hooked.

What is going to hook you in your retirement? Something will, if you create the opportunity for it to do so. It won't find you. You have to go find it. You may have to humble yourself to kind of start off at the kindergarten level. You will need a coach. You will need to study. You will need to practice. You may fail. At this point in your life, who cares? What matters is the trying.

If I can accomplish one thing with this book, I would want to convince you to not make retirement just an extension of your existing life. My wish for you is that you are just beginning an adventure. That you give it every effort to say yes to some things you've always avoided up to this point. Break new ground. Break through some barriers that *you* erected. Make yourself uncomfortable for a while, long enough to see if the risk is worth the reward. You get only this one life (near as I can tell). Don't leave some of the most interesting possible parts of it on the "I-wish" board. If you wish it, you can do it.

"Anything I've ever done that was ultimately worthwhile initially scared me to death."

Betty Bender

CHAPTER TWENTY-SEVEN

DO WHAT YOU THINK YOU CAN'T

"Most people live and die with their music still unplayed. They never dare to try."

Mary Kay Ash

I spent my whole adult life assessing risk. Here is what I know about risk.

- You can quantify risk with statistics and build odds from them. You can use those odds to help you make decisions—good ones. Do not ignore the stats.

- You do better when dealing with risk when you have experts around to help you both assess and mitigate it.

- Everything is risky.

- Five-hundred-year events can, and do, happen tomorrow or later this afternoon. In other words, even remotely expected events can jump up and surprise you. Just because it is a remote chance does not mean you can skip a backup plan, should the worst happen. Bad things can happen to good people.

- You cannot fully eliminate risk in most cases.

- Fear of risk will keep you from fully enjoying life or entering into potentially profitable business dealings.

- Handling risk has a lot to do with personal confidence. Lack of confidence may mean you won't be good at handling, or accepting, risk. That confidence can be built over time by those gutsy few who muster that first step of trying to venture outside of their comfort zones.

- You will only be able to fully handle risk once you take a chance and fail. It is the failing that really brings about the confidence. Survive breaking a leg, or losing some money, or something else horrific, and you find out that life goes on. Failures are setbacks, not stop signs.

By the way, letting fear rather than facts run your thinking is the cement that locks you into a timid life. Example: Most people are afraid of sharks. Heck, I am afraid of sharks. And yet, more people are killed by hot dogs, icicles, or deer each year than by sharks.

Linda and I do our best to study the risk involved in new adventures. We try our best to understand what can go wrong, and how that might take place. We consult or hire experts to give us advice, or even protect us. We stay alert to the possibilities. We try to have a backup plan and emergency supplies (with the notable exception of the C. J. disaster). We try to start off slow, and build our confidence. We have very few "absolutely-not" things we'll shy away from. We are open to adventure, and we completely realize it could all go tragically wrong. Such is life.

Here are a couple of examples I chose because they are "out there" a bit, and may serve to show how we handle risk.

- Linda and I went to Egypt before the revolution. We were there about a month. We saw Americans only once during our stay. We were in some remote and problematic locations. We did not dress like tourists. We kept to ourselves when warranted. We hired people with guns to protect us in a few places. We always had guides with us. We did back off of a couple of things we wanted to see because it was just too dangerous at the moment, like crossing the Sinai Peninsula, or going into the Sudan. We went to a few problematic places in the middle of the night with guards, because that was the safest time to visit. We drove though some areas behind tinted windows, because to do otherwise would have been taking unreasonable risk. I left a casino when a bunch of shouting started. Edgy trip, yes. But we stacked the odds heavily in our favor, took a lot of precautions, had a backup plan to get us out of Dodge at a moment's notice if we needed to (which would have cost us a bunch of money well-spent), did not take foolish risks, and listened to the advice of the experts we hired to keep us safe. Made it home in one piece, and loved the trip.

• Linda and I are in the ocean every day. Just about anyplace in the world with an ocean has sharks. Trust me on this. We knew that we would encounter them at certain places in Hawaii, and wanted to make sure we could handle those times without being terrified or hurt. So we started going out with shark experts, looking to participate right next to them in those encounters. Our first encounters were in the Bahamas with very mellow nurse sharks. We worked our way up to reef sharks, and that went well. We then went down to Mexico to get in with whale sharks that are 40 to 60 feet long (they eat only plankton), bull sharks, hammerheads, and others. Back to Hawaii to get comfortable with oceanic white-tips and tiger sharks. Each step along the way was a bit scary and a real rush. We found we were not in love with snorkeling with tiger sharks. We now knew how careful we had to be around oceanic white-tips. And we decided to draw the line at being outside the cage with great white sharks and orcas. We also learned how to stack the odds in our favor, and what not to do, like panic. Net result: We are now completely confident anywhere in the ocean, almost anyplace in the world, and we love swimming with sharks. And more recently, swimming with and photographing large crocodiles underwater off the Mexico/Belize border.

Daredevil? A bit. But that is not my point at all. I stacked the odds heavily in my favor in the above adventures. I did exercise caution and pretty good sense. I am comfortable now with going a bit further than most people would. I go nowhere near as far as my real daredevil friends here in Hawaii. And every single one of the adventures became a highlight of my life. I love them. I write about them.

One last quick story. My daughter-in-law, Sarah, came to visit. She is not 100 percent comfortable in the water. After a week, she had become more comfortable, and her confidence was up. Then she shocked me. She asked me to take her out for a night snorkel with the manta rays. Now, I've done this neat trip many times. But I can still remember my first time. You are in water that is 30 to 50-feet deep, in a place that any kind of shark might visit. It is night—dark as the inside of a cow. You jump off a boat into the water, and shine a light to attract plankton. The plankton come to the light. Pretty soon, manta rays arrive. They can be 10 to 15 feet across. They have huge mouths. They look very odd. They have a harmless stinger. They come right at you, then whirl in a circle to capture the plankton, sometimes gently bumping into you. Linda and I almost walked on water to get away from the first night manta we ever saw. However, within two minutes, we were back to breathing normally through our snorkels, and enjoying the experience to the extent of laughing out loud. We loved it. So did Sarah. After the manta swim, I asked her if she was afraid at any point. She admitted she was. I asked, "What scared you?" She said, "The European guy in the Speedo."

Fear faced is fear conquered, except when it comes to a European guy in a tiny Speedo.

"I don't want to be a passenger in my own life."

Diane Ackerman

CHAPTER TWENTY-EIGHT

THE JOYS OF A SECOND CAREER

"Find out what you like doing best and
get someone to pay you for doing it."

Katherine Whitehorn

I had no intention of taking on a second career. I put away enough money to make it to the finish line without going broke. I cherish my newfound freedom. I love being a sloth, having no plans for the day or week or month, not caring I don't know what time it is. I completely enjoy being able to accept an invitation without consulting my calendar, because I know there is nothing on it. I love not working. Don't miss anything about it except the occasional trip in the corporate jet, the great events I got to attend, and that lovely paycheck I got every two weeks. I love being retired. Love it.

I have no need whatsoever to conquer new worlds, build an empire, or become "important" again. None. Zero.

But a couple of things bugged me. One was that I had no place to show off my nifty photography work other than Facebook, which does present the images very well. The next was that my friends, C. J. and Nick, seemed stuck by their circumstances.

Their gallery was lovely, but small, and they could not show off their best images blown up in large sizes. It limited their income.

So, one weekend day when we were all hanging out at our place and swimming in the pool, I suggested that the three of us go up to the fanciest shopping center on the island, and see what a decent-sized gallery location might cost. Dead, stony silence. Now, I had attempted to move C. J. and Nick outside of their comfort zone. I gathered them up the next day, and we drove to see the space. I asked C. J. what he thought the gallery might look like in that space. He grabbed some paper from me and drew it out in about one minute. I asked him how he did that, and his reply was, "'Cause I've been designing this gallery in my mind for the past 10 years."

We leased the space. Each of us got one-third of the space. Linda and I shared our third. We drew up a one-paragraph business agreement. They run the gallery. I do some of the more complex business aspects. We agreed on how we would split the profits. And now, at the end of the month, we split the profits up like the communists we've become, without regard to who sold whose photo, or whether it came from the gallery or off the Web.

Next up, we decided to do a photo book together. Again, we all contributed our photos, and I did most of the work getting it ready for the design team and publisher. The book is now on sale in our galleries. We call it *The Hawaiian Collection*. It is absolutely beautiful, and we are all proud of it.

Looking to the future, we want to be in Waikiki. Waikiki has one of the busiest retail streets in America. Our products are a perfect fit for Waikiki. But we are going slow, and making sure that our existing businesses are highly profitable and our finances strong before we do further expansion. And there will be further photo books. We hope there will be *many* future books.

I always wanted to be an entrepreneur. Wanted to create jobs for people. Wanted to help create wealth for those I care about. Wanted a place where I could show off my work, and talk story with people about it on those few days that I choose to go into the gallery. Wanted to put my corporate skills to work in helping to design a small business. And I am not opposed to making good money doing it. Being in business again—one based on a passion of mine, with my wife and people I care about,—wow! Life is good.

It turns out that retirement is like Wednesdays on the old *Mickey Mouse Club* show. Wednesdays were "Anything Can Happen Day." If you leave yourself open to the possibilities, anything can, and will, happen.

And so—the joys of a second career. Quite the surprise.

> "Gentlemen, we are surrounded by insurmountable possibilities."

Pogo

CHAPTER TWENTY-NINE

THE NIGHTMARE OF A SECOND CAREER

"Be careful what you ask for, you might just get it."

Unknown

I never thought I would have a second career, and I really did not want anything in my life that even smelled like work. Ask my wife. I have literally hired people to clean our windows. I am anti-work at this point in my life. Been there, done that. I am over it completely.

Number one thing I want from my life: my freedom. Free to do any damn thing today that I want. Golf, surf, hike, photograph, and/or take a nap. I say "and/or" because I try to work a nap in there somewhere, no matter what else I do that day. Why? Because I can.

So now I have this second career. My agreement with the two guys is that neither Linda nor I need to work in the galleries, nor do we have any assigned or expected duties. How did I arrange such a good deal? First of all, Nick and C. J. get us. They understand what Linda and I both want out of our lives, because we told them. Second, I do provide some things of value to the venture. I handle some of the financing, much of the "business" stuff, I am a great negotiator, and I put that skill to work for the good of the venture. I've got some valuable contacts that have been useful to our business. We do our part as backup help when the galleries are short-handed. Linda has design skills that are useful, and we travel to bring home images from around the world that may sell well. We are good business associates, because we get out of the way of C. J. and Nick. They really know what they are doing in the gallery, unlike us. We don't need to be in the limelight of the gallery. We are smart enough to let C. J. and Nick be the face of the gallery. And the guys are smart enough to ask for help when they think we can provide it. It all works out very well.

So here comes the "nightmare" part.

Our business is a big success. We see that success growing as we expand our "brand" with new products and locations. I am the best (and only) one with the time to invest to check out these new possibilities. All of a sudden, I find myself at the airport, going places to meet with people. One of those meetings required me to wear shoes and a tie. Oh, the humanity. So, I scratch off an open-ocean swim with dolphins to meet people who have real jobs. You can begin to see the problem.

But there is more. It really takes all of us—C. J., Nick, Linda, and me—to launch anything new, build out another gallery, or design a coffee-table photo book. I'm not contracted to do this work, but I find I want and need to do it. Scratch off this evening's surf session.

And the worst is yet to come.

When I retired, I was extremely fortunate to have put away enough money to see me to the finish line. There was nothing foreseeable that could mess that up. There is now. You ought to see what the rent is in Waikiki. And leases are long, tying you to them for up to 10 years, at a whole bunch of money per month.

What if the economy tanks? What if there is war? What if SARS or Ebola or terrorism shuts down travel and keeps potential customers at home? What if one of us gets mad and leaves, or dies, or wants to venture off alone? All of a sudden, I have money at risk that I never wanted to put there. Heck, under just the right set of circumstances, this whole venture could reach deep into my retirement savings at age 70 or beyond. Kind of hard to recover from that kind of disaster.

So it is kind of a nightmare. But it really is just an extension of all the prior writing about risk-taking. I am not taking this second career risk without doing my homework, starting small, surrounding myself with experts, having backup plans, and stacking the odds in my favor. I am in charge of me. If I don't like how much time I am devoting to this venture, I will speak up and make some changes. And if it really doesn't work out, I will cut my losses, make some new plans, and life goes on.

In the meantime—wow. What a wonderful opportunity for Linda and me. So far, the second career is *way* more fun than the first, and I loved that one. And it has the potential of making me a lot more money than my first career, or hurting my finances. Either way, it will probably lead me to much more time at the beach. Right now, it kind of looks like work, with an asterisk. Work-lite, if you will.

> *"Your work is going to fill a large part of your life, and the only way to be truly satisfied is to do what you believe is great work. And the only way to do great work is to love what you do."*
>
> Steve Jobs

CHAPTER THIRTY

AND SPEAKING OF NIGHTMARES

The following falls into the category of "things I never really thought about."

I only recently got a really good, close-up look at what age does to a person. I am talking about people in their 80s and 90s. I will use my dad as an example.

My dad was the most competent person I ever met. At least, that was my view for about 60-some years. He had great jobs, was a terrific family man, a wonderful friend and neighbor, and had a whole bunch of nifty talents. He worked until age 70, with an important position on the team that built the B-2 stealth bomber. He and mom were married for 70 years. Dad was a complete man, and my idol.

One day in his 80s, he told me about some contracting work he was having done on the home. I could tell from 2,700 miles away that he was being scammed. He was. I then noticed that he couldn't really follow directions I was providing as we did FaceTime chats on the computer. Something was wrong.

What turned out to be wrong was that age jumped on my dad's back like a ton of bricks. By the time he was 90, he could barely stand, and he had lost so much weight that his pants would fall off when he did. He started multiple projects and finished none. His record-keeping became horrible. I stepped in as best I could to help him out. He died at 94. The last couple of years—not pretty.

Now my mom is in her mid-90s. I got her situated in a senior living place—not the easiest thing I've ever done. (You will figure out that I wrote the "Afterword" before deciding to do this chapter.) I then took over the family home, and started going through the papers and possessions.

My folks were raised during the Great Depression. The Depression was not a history lesson for them—it was their lives. Probably because of their shared experience, they saved everything. I found every Christmas card I sent them. A copy of every bill. Receipts for groceries bought in 1952. Advertisements and offers sent to them dating back to the 1950s. The stubs of every pencil they had ever owned, some just an eraser and a point of lead. You get the idea. A mess. By the way, our house was pretty much built in 1954 and never updated since then. On the few occasions when they were forced to replace carpet, linoleum, or the cover on a couch, you could find the old material out in our garage, right up until last week. Last week, all that stuff made its way to the dump under my supervision. Why bring this up? My dad and mom told me years ago that they had started to clean things out. They meant to do it. But age jumped on their backs before they got it done.

Oh, and by the way, they were going to nail down their exact senior living plans, or those for the surviving spouse. Well, that didn't happen either.

So, not griping about it, and happy to repay just a minor amount of the time they invested in me, all that stuff fell on my wife and me. So far, we've taken at least three months of our retirement toward handling mom and dad's (and my sister's, may she rest in peace) senior needs—finances, housing, and the like. My aunt Jeannie, an angel in western clothing, took more than two years of her life helping my folks and my mom deal with the issues of age.

And I forgot to mention the money thing. My parents own a valuable house, so that money will go toward helping my mom live out her life in comfort and safety. Good thing she has that house. Her senior living bills are about $7,000 to $8,000 a month, and will increase over time. Her Social Security and pension incomes are small. So what if living expenses for your mom or dad are $5,000 a month more than they can afford? Does that money come out of your pocket, or that of your brothers and sisters? I suggest you figure that out now, rather than later.

The point of this chapter is that not all things in retirement are fun and games. Dealing with aging parents or other loved ones may come your way. If you are like most people, you will be completely unprepared for this major challenge in your life. I strongly suggest you put together a game plan for dealing with these issues now, before age comes along and jumps on anyone's back. And while you are at it, put together a great plan for yourself and your spouse, so your kids need not make these important decisions for you.

AND ONE MORE THING TO WATCH OUT FOR WHILE WE ARE AT IT—ADDICTION

My editor, Bob Gorman, and I were recently discussing this book. He mentioned to me that he had been studying addiction and a related subject, post-traumatic stress disorder. Bob had issues that he had not dealt with, dating back to the Vietnam War and his participation in it. When he retired, he still had not dealt with those issues, but he did his best to deaden them with alcohol. That did not turn out well, and Bob finally got the help he needed. Today, he is sober, productive, and doing all he can to help others.

I am no expert in this field, but what Bob told me rang true. When some people lose the structure of their lives, they can become depressed, develop addictions, and generally lose their way. Now that I think back on it, one of the things I did as soon as I retired was to play professional poker, often in a casino, for 14 hours at a stretch. I played well and won money, but if that is not addiction, I do not know what is. I also played golf until my hands bled. Now, eight years into retirement, I am in a much better place, and merely take an average of 1,000 photos a day. Hey, maybe Bob is right about this addiction stuff.

So, my good friend and editor, Bob G., offered to write a chapter for me to add his advice on the subject of addiction and recovery, and I am glad he did. Here it is.

CHAPTER THIRTY-ONE

A CHAPTER FROM A FRIEND ABOUT ADDICTION AND RECOVERY

"I'm Bob, and I'm in recovery"—
a story you hope is never true about you.

By Bob G., Don's friend

This book has focused so far on planning—anticipating and acting on the retirement setting you envision to be true in the future, as best as you can see it now.

The retirement future is fueled largely by dollars and sense. So your *financial portfolio* is critical, and has been appropriately treated in these pages. But I want to suggest that there's an equally critical agenda to consider—your *social portfolio*. That will become the air that you breathe as you navigate through the years ahead, engaging with others, and both giving and receiving social nourishment along the way. More about this in a few paragraphs.

So as you think about your future, there are some things that aren't fun to anticipate, such as health concerns, or worse—end-of-life issues. There are many other books that address these extensively and effectively. This is not one of those books.

The best book I know that does help guide us in planning for the future we'd prefer not to have is *Being Mortal*, by Atul Gawande. It's about making choices and having conversations about them, and doing it sooner, rather than later. They are difficult "quality-of-life" choices and conversations. But you and your loved ones will help yourselves immeasurably by facing them ahead of the crisis, chaos, and confusion. The theme of the book is also covered in a PBS *Frontline* show called "Being Mortal." In one hour, you can get an overview of some of the issues all of us will face as we get older, our immune systems begin to weaken, and we start dealing with questions like: Do I really want to try the latest and greatest medical remedy if it only prolongs my life for more painful treatments? Is this about actually getting better, or just extending life without a real chance for returning to the way I want to live?

Continuing along this happy path, one issue that all of us would rather not face is the possibility of addiction, clinically called substance-abuse disorder. Here's one description of this malady. If you have tried repeatedly to limit the volume and/or frequency of your drinking (or drugging) and failed, you may have a problem. Unlike the diseases of diabetes or cancer that are diagnosed by professionals, only you can detect this disorder in yourself. Others might suggest that you have a problem, based on evidence like losing your job, home, marriage, and family. Or maybe it's a DUI. Maybe it's your self-respect. With this disease, only you can diagnose it. And in so doing, you have the opportunity to recognize that you need help, and maybe even step up and get it.

Why is substance abuse a subject for *this* book? Shouldn't this just be about happy things? Ideally, yes. Practically, no. Retirement can change a lot more than getting a steady paycheck.

When some of us move from a very structured life with fixed hours, established places, social context, and related spiritual nourishment, it can be a struggle. Some choose to numb the pain and discomfort with chemicals like alcohol, but also include prescription drugs, cocaine, heroin, and crystal meth.

Why do we choose artificial remedies rather than talking to others about our fears, concerns, and worries for the future, and just getting through today and tonight?

Author Brene Brown says that the reason we are here at all is to form and maintain connections with others. This is simply harder to do in the midst of large-scale change. When we miss the connections we are used to having, and that have nourished us, sometimes we substitute drugs and alcohol. They can provide a temporary salve for the loneliness and desperation that can surround and overwhelm us in retirement. But sooner or later, they bring unpleasant, sometimes life-threatening consequences.

I know. I went from 25 years of corporate structure in a Fortune 50 company to working by myself in one day. No transition. I didn't know how much I would miss the boring meetings and stupid agendas that filled my days for all of those years. Did I mention the awful lunches? I left the corporate world and set up my own business, working from home. I traded being around people all day to being by myself.

I had no idea that, in deciding to leave the corporate world, I would also be stepping into a realm for which I was totally unprepared. This was a world of isolation, cut off from friends, family, and potential well-wishers. Hanging out solo in my office basement was almost the beginning of the end.

When my consulting business was busy, I was OK. When things got quiet, I became afraid. And the drinking I had done in the past accelerated in its frequency and volume. If I tell you that

I drank in the morning, I think that would say it clearly enough. I was out of control. Just ask my wife, Linda. I had many episodes in which I embarrassed or hurt myself, and worst of all, injured the ones I love the most.

One example. At this point in the slow and steady decline into literally becoming someone else, my day centered around drinking instead of working, spending time with others, and doing things that I otherwise love, like reading and fishing. Things at home were unpleasant. Linda realized that she wasn't going to change me, despite her best efforts. Our relations were frosty. Let's just say that there wasn't much happy interaction in our home for several years.

Linda now tells the story of having a recurring nightmare. She would hear the doorbell ring in the middle of the night. She would get up and answer the door, only to find another woman looking in, sobbing uncontrollably. Through her tears, she asked, "Why did you let your husband drive drunk and kill my son? Why?"

I was lucky that this nightmare never actually happened. But that wasn't because I didn't drive drunk. I did. Many times. I just never hit another car and driver. There were no deaths. But there easily could have been. I never killed anyone else, but I was doing a good job on me.

Linda's recurring nightmare is one example of my selfishly stealing serenity from her.

Fueled by alcohol, I became someone else. And he wasn't someone you'd like to spend time with—self-absorbed, short-tempered, and insufferable.

It took a lot of wreckage in my personal life for me to acknowledge, admit, and accept that I needed help. My efforts to control (limit) my drinking failed repeatedly. I sought help. I became part of a 12-Step Program, and enrolled in addiction treatment at a hospital. I stopped and started drinking many times before I got it. I have been sober about four years. You don't recover from this disease. You just get daily immunity from it *if* you keep doing the things that got you sober in the first place. It's like a diabetic taking insulin. Yes, every day.

Everyone has a story. That's part of mine. Only you know your story, and whether or not you have a problem. Unfortunately, self-diagnosis of substance-abuse disorder is a very slippery slope. No one wants to admit there is a problem, especially when it's something so pervasive that affects how you live your life and behave toward others, and how they treat you.

Stepping up and saying that I'm an alcoholic or drug addict isn't at the top of my list of things I want to do today. I don't want it on my resume, or included in my eulogy. And yet, I freely admit that, in my humanity, I'm imperfect. And as the treatment facilitators like to say, "That's OK."

Accordingly, while I was still on the quest for a substance-free life, and not doing particularly well at it, I became a master of denial, delusion, and deception. Beyond telling myself that I didn't have a problem despite the large path of destruction I left behind me, I also hid bottles and cans. I kept redefining what "normal" drinking meant. Because if I wasn't a normal (social) drinker, that would make me an alcoholic. Now I can see that when I was drinking, I wasn't acting in my own self-interests. I was also killing myself on every level possible. But I couldn't see that back then, let alone begin to change it. Because that would mean I'd have to change. And as someone once said, "No one likes change except a wet baby."

But it's change that we sometimes need. If we have lost the connections and closeness that we need as humans to survive and thrive, it's time to do something we are hard-wired not to want to do: *Ask for help.*

I now work with veterans—women and men returning from Iraq and Afghanistan, some still trying to come home from Vietnam. These "older individuals" like me unpacked their bags when they landed back on U.S. soil 40-plus years ago. But some have never been able to unpack their emotions and re-engage with the world they left behind when they entered the service. It's time. We need everyone back. Time to come home.

Some of these veterans get lost in addictions. Some get in trouble with the law. They have all sorts of reasons to raise their hands and ask for help. But the military culture teaches them to keep marching through their pain. Suck it up. Don't be a wimp. Don't display anything that might resemble weakness or vulnerability. So they don't ask for help. Not only do *they* suffer. So do their families. One horrible effect—domestic abuse shows its ugly face. As a society, we become weaker for everyone we lose like this.

I like to say, *Real heroes ask for help.*

So if you see yourself in the copy above, do us all a favor, and be a hero today. Do what's best for you. It will make your retirement—and life—full of the great experiences that are out there, just waiting for you to embrace.

CHAPTER THIRTY-TWO

LET GO OF THE THINGS
THAT SUCK JOY FROM YOUR LIFE

*"The less you respond to negative people,
the more peaceful your life will be."*

Unknown

Now that I am retired, I have lots more time to look at my emails and things like Facebook. First of all, I have very few emails, so it is possible for me to actually read all of them. And I love Facebook, where I am amazed at how fantastic some of my friends' lives appear to be, and astonished at the pain so many people suffer.

So, in the old days, I just quickly deleted all forwarded emails en masse. I had no time for them. In retirement, I can open up the emails and see what they contain. Most are from friends my age. Many of them are retired. It would appear than not one of them was ever in the business of fact-checking. It would also appear that they endorse every kind of lie, half-truth, no truth, unfair, hateful, race-baiting, fear-mongering, ignorant message ever posted on electronic media. Worse yet, they want me to pass this trash along to all my friends, that is, if I am a truly patriotic American. If I am just some kind of run-of-the-mill, commie-pinko America-hater, I can go ahead, and be a coward and delete the email.

First, the messages made my blood boil. I mean, how dare the president sell off all the energy assets of our country to his Muslim friends for a one-time payment of only one dollar? How dare they plan to raid all of our homes on a Thursday night to take away our guns and then put us in jail for treason? How dare they make it mandatory that all marriages be between two people of the same sex? Not on my watch.

Then I started looking at these messages. Did me a little research. Seems like parts of these missiles of truthfulness strayed partially from the strictest fact. Turns out most of them were complete and absolute bullshit.

So now I was mad again. Why would my friend want to embarrass or try to fool me? Why, indeed.

I had a couple of discussions with the senders about their emails. Those conversations went nowhere.

So, I could do one of three things: join the fun and forward the lies, drop my friends like hot potatoes, or say I love them, but please take me off their forward list. I chose the third one. My life is now a whole lot better.

We all get around a bunch of people who hate the government, the police, the military, some other race or religion, welfare taxes, war—well, you know who I am talking about. I watch them get red in the face when they hit on these subjects. Today, I don't let it pass. I ask whether all this political discussion is making them happy. They all admit that it is not. I then tell them that it doesn't make me happy, either, and I don't want to participate in it. Some of them get it, and others don't. I stopped hanging out much with the ones that don't.

A lot of what you become in retirement will be influenced by those with whom you spend time. If they want to wallow in the poop of our nation's politics, roll them out of my eyesight. I want nothing to do with it. Put me in with some really ignorant, happy people. We will get along just fine.

"I don't have time to be negative."

Venus Williams

CHAPTER THIRTY-THREE

IF SOMETHING IS NOT WORKING, CHANGE IT.

"When you are finished changing, you are finished."

Benjamin Franklin

This is your time. You are in charge. No one is telling you what to do. You have no excuses. You need no justification. Go for it.

My unobjective observation is that most people just extend the life they have directly into retirement. Like I said earlier, maybe they winter someplace warm. Maybe they don't work as many hours or labor at a tough job. But in large part, their lives have barely changed. Oh, they travel more now. They take river cruises and railroads and big buses across Europe. They volunteer more. But life goes on much as before.

If that is going to be your life, God bless you. That is your choice. That it would not be my choice, who cares. None of my business. What is important is whether or not you are really happy. If you are not feeling the joy of retirement every single day, the kind that says, "Thank God for our retirement, our good health, these fun things we are doing. Man, I love living here!," well, it is all on you. You are the CEO of your retired life. Change something! Bust a move.

DON'T SETTLE! If you find yourself saying, "My life would be perfect if we didn't have to put up with this cold weather from December to April," stop doing it. Move! Get the heck out of there. Go to where the sun shines.

If you find yourself depressed for weeks on end, do something about it. Depression is one wicked son of a bitch, and I hope anyone suffering from it gets professional help. The first step: Do something positive about it. Talk to someone who can help you.

If you find yourself saying, "Gee, I sure wish I could do that," go for it. What is stopping you?

When it comes right down to it, your retirement happiness is not based on money or circumstances. It is based on your willingness to have fun with what you have. I have a lot of buddies at the beach who have basically zero. Some even use cafeteria lunch trays as body surfing tools. And I get to see them smile every single day. If you are not thrilled with your retirement, keep making changes until you are. You deserve it.

"Age is something that does not matter, unless you are a cheese."

Bill Burke

CHAPTER THIRTY-FOUR

WHY DID I CHOOSE SUCH A
HORRIBLE TITLE FOR THIS BOOK?

The title of this book is *Smells Like Retirement*. I chose that title, because there is a smell to retirement. Some smell like a grandparent's basement. Some smell like a stagnant pond. Some smell like a new car. Others smell tropical. The smell you get is what you put together for yourself. You choose the fragrance. You launch the spray. It is of your design and making. A happy retirement is entirely up to you.

AFTERWORD

As I finish off this manuscript, I am rushing a bit so I can catch a plane to the Mainland to help my 95-year-old mother transition into an assisted living facility. This is, emotionally, one of the toughest things I've done in my entire life. Mom loves her home, is comfortable there, and would like to stay until her last days. However, she needs the kind of help now that she can get only in a more structured environment, so the time is right.

I bring this up, because I have only one chapter on the realities of aging, and I think you deserve a better preview of what is ahead. So here we go.

I think you will be kind of shocked at how quickly you may age as you hit 65 and beyond. I just attended my 50th high school reunion. I promise you, we looked better at the prom. Age is a bitch.

I will speak for myself. Everyone will have a somewhat different experience.

- My eyesight has gone to hell—kind of a problem for a photographer.

- My hearing is horrible. And at the same time, my wife's hearing seems to be improving. The difference in hearing abilities causes friction. My hearing loss makes me want to avoid hard-to-hear events like dinners in loud restaurants or, frankly, anything involving, you know, words or sound.

- I was an all-American sprinter. I really can't run at all anymore. I can speed up, but I cannot run. Horrifying.

- I have one thing lost at all times. Most are eventually found. But I am always misplacing something.

- I have less drive to get anything done. This from a Type-A, hard-charging guy. Shocking to me.

- I look like hell. I have things showing up on my skin that I did not know could grow on people. I've had a bunch of me cut out, frozen off, or chemically removed.

- My hair is a joke and beyond repair. I scare little children without trying.

- I love to work out, but now when I do, I injure myself. You think that you can work around that and keep right on rolling? Good luck. My six-pack is now a keg.

- I dress like a bum (and love it).

On a more upbeat note, I do more to keep myself well-groomed and up-to-date with what is going on in the world. I don't want to be the old guy with the giant wad of hair coming out of his ears or nose, or who has no idea who Taylor Swift is, or how the "Interweb" works. Oh, and I am the happiest I've ever been in my life and *by far* the most relaxed.

All that said, I can see where this is headed. So, we have done a few things you might want to consider.

- We have all of our important papers like wills, powers of attorney, trusts, and instructions upon death up-to-date, and posted on a website where our kids and others with permission can access them.

- We have our burial plans well-lined-out for others to handle with a minimum of work.

- Our kids know where to find our assets and what they are.

- We have enough money to take care of us in an assisted living environment, either in our own home or at a facility. I mention this, because those costs can be up to $10,000 a month per person. That's right. I checked them out in two states and found that, for an individual who needs memory care, perhaps because of dementia, monthly costs are about $10,000. Heck, even if the person doesn't need that degree of care, the monthly costs can be $4,000 to $7,000. So, time for you to start thinking about how you will pay that for your dad or mom, or yourself, when the time comes. Do you need long-term-care insurance? Are there government programs available that can help you? Better check it out.

- I mentioned earlier that we are doing the best we can to whittle down our worldly goods to the bare minimum. Really hard, but it must be done. What do you really want to leave for others? What do you not care about at all? Decide now, while you still can.

- We are getting all the medical assistance possible. One thing we know for sure. If you have any kind of a medical problem, and put off addressing it, the issue will turn into a really big deal. It may even kill you sooner, rather than later. I urge you to keep on top of your health. Never, ever give up on it.

- We've forgiven a few bastards that really don't deserve it. But we have found the cost of carrying forward the hatred to be just too high. I am currently pissed off at no one, not mad about anything, and pretty doggone happy in my little delusional world.

- I've made sure those I love know it. I've told them so plainly, and with emotion.

- I'm good with my faith in God.

- I am good with the fact that the issue is not *if* I will eventually die, but *when*. If that happens in my sleep, cool. If it happens in the jaws of a tiger shark, I'm good with that. I would prefer the sleep option.

- I am one thankful son of a gun. Thankful for each and every day.

And so it goes. Age creeps along. Things are perfect. Perfect. Oops, that's a problem. Oh, shit. What now? Prepare as best you can, and live each day to the fullest. Overall, the best days of my life, so far.

I loved my charge up the ladder of life. Loved surviving. Loved thriving. Loved the wins, and hated the losses. Got to where I thought I was a pretty valuable human being, and felt I was central to the success of organizations and a whole circle of people. I was right about the first part. I was, and I am, a highly valuable human being, and so are you. But "central to the success of organizations and a whole circle of people"—not so much. Not so much that they couldn't find a way to get along without me. And they have done so magnificently. Life goes on. There are fun things ahead. Let's go find them.

ACKNOWLEDGEMENTS

I want to thank my webpage designer, Steve Bennett, of Author-Bytes, for causing me to abandon an already written book on supervision and management, and to then write another on changing one's life. The world did not need another advice book on how to supervise and manage. I never liked that book much, anyway. I threw it away.

Steve also taught me how to think visually, rather than verbally or in writing. Took him about three minutes to do so, and it really helped me out. Thanks, Steve.

I wrote the book that Steve helped me to visualize, on changing your life from what you have, to what you want, completed it, and sent it to my friend and highly successful author, Dr. Dan Tomal.

Dr. Dan was extremely gracious in his praise of the writing, but pointed out a few flaws for me to consider. I suspect I already knew the flaws were there and just needed some honest feedback before I dealt with them. After re-reading his comments, and thinking about how much I would have to change that book, I packaged up the manuscript and put it in the back of my closet, where it sits to this day. I came to hate that book, and I am very thankful that I did not go forward with it. Dan was right on in his comments, and saved me from putting out a highly unfocused book. Google Dr. Daniel Tomal, Ph.D., to find out his contact information, and the amazing body of work he has completed. Dan is a remarkable man.

Then, a year ago, I had dinner with an old friend of mine, Doug Holtz. Doug and I had both served at different times as national president of the Society of Chartered Property and Casualty Underwriters (CPCU)—a professional organization with about 22,000 members. In fact, the year I was president, Doug served on my board. Doug is nearing retirement age, and I asked him his plans. He had not yet given it a lot of thought. I mentioned I had about five chapters written (in the book I hate, but I did like these) that I thought might be of interest to him. He asked me to send them. I did. He liked them, but felt they didn't answer a couple of critical questions for him. So I banged out a chapter-length email on the subject and sent it to him. He liked it so much that he encouraged me to write a book on the subject. About a week later, due in part to the head start of having five key chapters already done, I produced my first draft of this book.

My good friend, Mary Lovein, owner of the Holualoa Gallery on the Big Island, has been a big supporter of mine. She was the first to sell my photographic images in her gallery. She was also the first to read the rough draft of this book, and provided me with great input and encouragement. Much thanks, Mary.

The people who taught me the lessons, ideas, and concepts that show up throughout this book are so numerous that I could never name them all. Teachers, coaches, mentors, co-workers, authors, and lecturers, along with websites and books. I will name a few.

My parents, Jim and Coleen Hurzeler, who got me thinking about saving up for retirement before I even started working.

Coach O'Rourke, God rest his soul, from my track and field days at Palos Verdes High School. Coach taught me about discipline, planning, and pushing myself into areas I didn't really want to explore, because I was afraid of the pain, the possibility of injury, and of failing. Places like running the hurdles and the

400 meters, and workouts that would kill off a good horse. All his lessons have served me well to this day.

Coach Steve Simmons, my Chapman University coach. Steve is still teaching me. He, too, pushed me way outside of my comfort zone. He let me win, fail, and have fun along the way. He taught me more about diversity than he will ever know. And Steve is near the center of one of the greatest stories of sportsmanship ever to happen on this earth. Allow me a brief aside to tell that story.

In 1968, two athletes on our U.S.A. Olympic Track and Field Team shocked the world by raising their arms and bowing their heads while on the stand, accepting their Olympic gold and bronze medals. The national anthem was playing. Tommy Smith and John Carlos were thrown off the team, and out of Olympic Village. The shame of it all.

Times change. Years later, Tommy and John are, in many parts of America, considered to be heroes. On the campus of San Jose State University in California, there is a statue representing them on the victory stand in Mexico City. They are sought-after speakers, and now highly honored elder statesmen.

The little-known story is that there was a third person on the stand with them—silver medalist, Peter Norman, of Australia. Tommy and John told him what they were about to do shortly before the ceremony. Peter asked if he could join them, as he had strong feelings about the way Aboriginal people had been treated in his home country. Tommy and John asked that he not join them. This was their moment. Peter then asked if he could wear a badge in support of Aboriginal people, and they all agreed. Peter's wearing the badge went pretty much unnoticed around the world, but it did not play well in Australia. Peter suffered the consequences back home.

Fast-forward to 2010. Peter died. He, too, had been honored during his later years. Society had caught up with his point of view. Now here comes the great part. My coach, an African-American, Steve Simmons, joined up with Tommy Smith and John Carlos to fly to Australia to carry the casket of their friend and competitor, Peter Norman, to his final finish line. Even writing this piece brings tears to my eyes. I have never been so proud of my coach or athletes in general. Steve continues to show me how to live a life of honor and respect.

I want to thank every chief financial officer I've ever known for helping me to have a good understanding of money, and how it works. Same for the actuaries I've worked with for helping me to understand risk and statistics. And special thanks to all my economics teachers, who taught me how/why things get produced, distributed, priced, and sold.

Loretta Malandro shaped much of my thinking about communications and relationships. You ought to pick up some of her books. She is an excellent communicator. Check out her website at www.malandro.com. If you get any one of her books, you will end up reading all of them. Time well-spent.

I've already mentioned C. J. Kale and Nick Selway, two guys who are still changing my life for the better, each and every day. They own two photo galleries, one in Kailua-Kona, Hawaii, and the other in Waikoloa Queens Market Place, on the Big Island of Hawaii. I am proud to have my images for sale in these two galleries. Check out LavaLightGalleries.com.

My wife, Linda, for always encouraging me to write, and giving me the space to do it, along with some great shoulder massages to help me with my typing.

Thanks also to Hal Bennett for reading my first draft and making some great suggestions. And to my long-time editor and forever friend, Bob Gorman, for his review, continued support, and the chapter he let me include on addiction and recovery. I am proud of you, Bob, and thankful to have you as my friend.

My abundant thanks, as well, to the team of professionals who do the hard and exacting work needed to bring this book to both print and e-book publication. Kua Bay Publishing, LLC is basically me. But behind that little curtain are the folks who do the real work to bring the book to market. They edit, design the cover and the layout of the book and then do whatever is needed to get it in print and online. Specifically, Steve Bennett at AuthorBytes® and his team, including the lead on this book, Dan Snow. Thank you for getting this book completed and ready to fly.

ABOUT THE AUTHOR

Don Hurzeler is retired. He was born in 1947, started work full-time in 1969, and retired in 2008. He and his wife, Linda, live in Kailua-Kona, Hawaii. They have two grown children and four growing grandchildren.

Along the way, Don graduated from Chapman University, where he is a member of their Athletic Hall of Fame. He earned 1969 NCAA Division Two All-American status as a sprinter/hurdler. Don had a nearly 40-year insurance career, during which he rose to chief underwriting officer for Zurich U.S. and CEO/president of Zurich Middle Markets. Don was also president of the Zurich Foundation, and served on the board of directors for American Nuclear Insurers.

Don is a Chartered Property and Casualty Underwriter (CPCU) and a Chartered Life Underwriter (CLU). He served as the 2004-2005 national president of the National Society of CPCU—at the time, an organization of 25,000 members.

Don has authored two previous books, *Designated for Success* (2004), and *The Way Up: How to Keep Your Career Moving in the Right Direction* (2010). *The Way Up* won the gold medal for Career Book of the Year from Axiom Business Book Awards. Don was a columnist for newspapers and magazines, and a contributing writer for other authors, Web services, and news outlets.

In the last few years, Don has concentrated his efforts on doing any damn thing he chooses. He's *retired*. One of the things he chose to do was to become a photographer. Don was coached by noted landscape photographers, C. J. Kale and Nick Selway. He eventually won awards for his photography, and started selling his images in the Lava Light Galleries on the Big Island of Hawaii. You can view his and Linda's images at http://donhurzeler.smugmug.com.

In 2015, Don worked with C. J. Kale, Nick Selway, Linda Hurzeler, ICLA, and TEN:AM Design to publish a coffee-table book of images titled *The Hawaiian Collection*. This book is available at www.lavalightgalleries.com.

Check out www.donhurzeler.com for more information about Don and his various projects.

Made in the USA
Lexington, KY
22 November 2019